Path to the
Anglo-Saxon Paganism

by Swain Wódening

This book is dedicated to my son in hopes that he will have many others to worship with in the future.

Copyright ©2012 Berry Canote

Published in the United States of America by Wednesbury Shire, Huntsville, MO

Edited by Jeff Wolf

Cover art and design by Saga Erickson

Table of Contents

Foreword 1
What is Anglo-Saxon Paganism? 5
Who were the Anglo-Saxons? 10
Gods, Goddesses, and Other Beings 17
    What is a God? 17
    Wóden 19
    Fríge 21
    Þunor 22
    Tiw 23
    Ing 24
    Fréo 26
    Hama 26
    Neorð 27
    Neorðu 27
    Ėostre 28
    Hreda 29
    Seaxnéat 30
    Helið 30
    The Ancestors 31
    Elves, Cofgodas, and Other Beings 35
Key Concepts 39
    Wyrd 39
    The Sacred and The Holy 41
    Inneryard and Outeryard 43
    Frith 44
    Frith and Law 46
    Grith 49
Thews 50
    Wisdom 50
    Worthmind or Honor 51
    Weathdeal or Generosity 51
    Bravery 54
    Industriousness 55
    Hospitality 56
    Loyalty 57
    Truth 57

- Friendship 58
- Moderation 59
- Neighborliness 60
- Steadfastness 60

Rites 61
- Ritual Tools 61
- Altar Dedication 61
- Composing a Prayer 64
  - The Outline 64
  - Composition in English and Old English 67
  - Composing a Prayer 69
- Making Offerings 70
  - The Purpose of Offering 71
  - Offerings in Ancient Times 74
  - Offerings in Modern Times 78
- Symbel 81
  - The Order of Symbel 84
  - Some Rules for Symbel 86
  - A Few More Words on Symbel 87
- Conclusion 87

Holy Tides 88
- Yule 88
  - Módraniht 89
  - Twelve Days of Yule 96
  - Other Yule Traditions 98
- Solmónaþ 99
- Hredmónaþ 102
- Éosturmónaþ 103
- Sumerdæg 107
- Liða 109
- Hláfmæst 112
- Háligmónaþ 114
- Winterfylleþ 116
- Conclusion 118

Endword 119
Glossary 121
Suggested Reading List 126
Bibliography 128

Foreword

Before we begin, you need to know a few things. The Anglo-Saxons were a group of tribes that invaded what is now England about 1500 years ago. Our language English is descended from theirs; anyone of English descent is descended from them. English-speaking countries owe much of their culture to the Anglo-Saxons. They were considered Germanic tribes, that is, they spoke languages related to modern English, German, Dutch, Swedish, Danish, and Norwegian (these are all Germanic languages). A pagan is anyone that is not Christian, Muslim, or Jew. Paganism is any religion that owes nothing to Christianity, Islam, or Judaism. Pagan religions tend to have many gods and goddesses. Anglo-Saxon paganism is often called Anglo-Saxon Heathenry. Heathen is another word for pagan, and heathenry is another word for paganism.

This is not the first book on modern Anglo-Saxon paganism, or even the second. The first was my book "Hammer of the Gods: Anglo-Saxon Paganism in Modern Times." When I wrote "Hammer of the Gods: Anglo-Saxon Paganism in Modern Times" almost ten years ago. I never dreamed the success it would have. Between it and its second edition it has sold over two thousand copies. This is quite phenomenal for a book with such a small audience. However, one complaint that often came up was that it was too advanced for those just starting out in Anglo-Saxon paganism. It assumed that one already knew of Anglo-Saxon paganism, and knew a bit about it. At the time it first saw print, this was not a problem. Most folks were coming from a background in Asatru (pronounced Ahsa-true), the related religion based on that of the Vikings, and therefore were already familiar with many of the concepts, myths, and virtues, and only needed them put in an Anglo-Saxon pagan perspective. Therefore, there was no need for a glossary, or to explain things in simple terms. The only need there was, was to give the reader an Anglo-Saxon Heathen viewpoint.

Since then, things have changed. Many, if not most folks coming to Anglo-Saxon paganism are coming from different backgrounds with only the barest of knowledge concerning the old pagan religions. Thus, this book is meant to meet the need for something simple and straightforward.

This book is a book meant for beginners. It is not meant to be a scholarly work. You will not find citations for the sources unless it is something directly quoted. Almost all of "Path to the Gods..." is common knowledge to one that has been practicing Anglo-Saxon paganism for some time. If one wishes a book that provides extensive citations, or something more advanced, they are advised to pick up a copy of the second edition of "Hammer of the Gods: Anglo-Saxon Paganism in Modern Times." You are encouraged after reading this book, to pick up a copy of that work anyway.

From this book you will learn what Anglo-Saxon paganism is. You will learn that it is a polytheistic religion, one that has many gods and goddesses. You will learn that Anglo-Saxon paganism has no creed, but relies instead on custom and tradition. You will learn who the Anglo-Saxons were and why they are relevant to today's English-speaking world. You will learn what a god is, that a god is a very powerful spirit that seeks to help Mankind, and who the Anglo-Saxon pagan gods and goddesses are. You will learn about wyrd, and how it determines the path of your life. You will learn the virtues of Anglo-Saxon paganism. Finally, you will learn how to perform the rites of Anglo-Saxon paganism, and the holy times to perform them on. If you do not learn these things, then I have not done my job as a writer, and I profusely apologize. If you already know them, then I hope I have not bored you with repetition.

I first became interested in Germanic Heathenry when I was in the third grade. I had read a book called "The Secret Hide-Out." In it was a club called the Viking Club. This led me to look up the word Viking in the encyclopaedia. I was hooked. From there I began to read about the Vikings and their gods. I came to Anglo-Saxon Heathenry in 1989 when I was 26. I had been Asatru for about four years, and wished to follow a religion more closely to that of my English and Saxon ancestors. At the time, the number of Anglo-Saxon pagans could be counted on one's fingers and toes. Indeed, I did not come in contact with other Anglo-Saxon pagans other than my brother until 1993 when I learned of Garman Lord and Gert McQueen members of an Anglo-Saxon pagan group called the Wínland (pronounced winland) Ríce (pronounced reech-a). For many years there were not many Anglo-Saxon pagans, but as the Wínland Ríce grew, there was more and more interest in Anglo-Saxon paganism. In 1996, Winifred Hodge Rose and I founded the Anglo-Saxon Ealdriht, and in a few years, Anglo-Saxon Heathenry exploded. By the time the Ealdriht dissolved in 2004 there were hundreds of Anglo-Saxon pagans. In 2003, "Hammer of the Gods: Anglo-Saxon Paganism in Modern Times" was published further spurring the growth of Anglo-Saxon paganism. There are now over thirty-three Anglo-Saxon pagan groups with hundreds if not thousands of adherents to Anglo-Saxon paganism. Needless to say the growth of Anglo-Saxon paganism has been phenomenal.

With all this growth, I saw a need for a more basic book, one that someone that has never heard of the Anglo-Saxons would be able to pick up, and begin practicing Anglo-Saxon paganism. It is hoped this book will be simple enough that anyone can understand, yet advanced enough to give one a firm grounding in the beliefs of the modern Anglo-Saxon pagan. In the back of the book you will find a glossary with many of the more foreign terms defined. Also there you will find a pronunciation guide to help with pronouncing many of the Old English (Old English was the language of the Anglo-Saxons) words used in this book. Along the way I try to provide pronunciations for many of the names and words you may not be familiar with. Finally, there is a reading list (in addition to a bibliography) that will lead you to other books to read about Anglo-Saxon paganism.

This book is the way I practice Anglo-Saxon paganism. It is not the way necessarily that other Anglo-Saxon pagans practice, or even perhaps that of the majority. It is my own way, and is based on years of research into the old religion, and the practice of it by others and myself. There are many different ways folks practice Anglo-Saxon paganism, and if you ask ten Anglo-Saxon pagans how they practice Anglo-Saxon paganism, you are likely to get ten different answers. Never the less, it is hoped this book can be of use to you. When finished, you are encouraged to read Alaric Albertsson's "Travels Through Middle Earth: The Path of a Saxon Pagan," if you have not already, and then my other book on the topic "Hammer of the Gods: Anglo-Saxon Paganism in Modern Times." A final note I use the words man, men, Man, and Mankind in a neuter sense. If I wish to specify a member of the male sex I use the term wermen.

Swain Wódening
Hreðmonað, 1563 wintra siððan Englan tocyme.
March 2012

What is Anglo-Saxon Paganism?

Anglo-Saxon paganism goes by many names. Perhaps the most common is Anglo-Saxon Heathenry (called ASH for short). Others call it Ésatréow (pronounced roughly ace-uh-tray-ow), Fyrnsidu (pronounced roughly furn-sid-eww), Saxon Paganism amongst others. Ésatréow means "faith in the gods," while Fyrnsidu means "the old ways." Both are very descriptive of Anglo-Saxon paganism. Anglo-Saxon pagans rely on their gods very much in their daily lives. They develop relationships with them, and give gifts to them in return for the help they give. So "faith in the gods" is a good way to describe Anglo-Saxon paganism. "The old ways" is also a good way to describe Anglo-Saxon paganism. Ancient Anglo-Saxon pagans had no word for their religion, and instead referred to it as sidu "custom or tradition." The word Heathen comes from Old English *hæðen*, a word whose origin has been stated by scholars as a native word related to Greek *ethnos* "nation, race" or a gloss for Latin *paganus* "rural dweller" meaning "dweller on the heath." The word pagan comes from Latin *paganus*. Rural dwellers were the last to convert when Christianity came to Europe. Therefore, words for a rural dweller came to mean those that followed any of the old religions that had many gods and goddesses. Today, a pagan or heathen is anyone that is not Christian, Muslim, or Jew. Heathen in the last twenty or so years has come to mean one that follows the Germanic gods and goddesses specifically.

Anglo-Saxon paganism is a religion based on that of the ancient Anglo-Saxons (who will be covered in the next chapter). It is a polytheistic religion, that is, it has many gods and goddesses. It is also a reconstructed religion. A reconstructed religion is a religion that died out, but now has been reconstructed or revived by researching the beliefs and practices of an ancient people that have survived in texts and through archaeological finds. Reconstruction is done using scholarly standards. Heathen scholars use the same standards that are applied by university researchers. The idea is to reconstruct the worldview of an ancient pagan people, and then try to practice what we have learned from that reconstructed worldview. This has required many years of work by many folks looking into the beliefs and practices of the ancient Anglo-Saxon pagans. Many Anglo-Saxon pagans regularly read scholarly books and journals to gain insight into ancient pagan practices and beliefs. When you are through with this book you may want to read many of the scholarly works as well. Because Anglo-Saxon paganism is a reconstructed religion, there are many different ways to follow Anglo-Saxon paganism. Just as there are many different opinions amongst scholars, there are many different ways to practice Anglo-Saxon Heathenry.

Why reconstruct a religion though to worship the Anglo-Saxon gods? Couldn't we just make up rites or adapt rites from other religions? Well, the reason is that the ancient Anglo-Saxons knew much more about the gods and the rites to worship them than we do. They were raised in the faith of the Anglo-Saxon gods and learnt the virtues of an Anglo-Saxon pagan at a very young age. An ancient ten-year-old Anglo-Saxon pagan child probably knew more about being an Anglo-Saxon pagan than the most experienced Anglo-Saxon pagan living today. In order to learn what the ancient Anglo-Saxon pagans knew about how to worship the gods, and behave as an upstanding Heathen, we must reconstruct their worldview. Sure, we could just make up rites to worship the gods, and through trial and error find out what works best, but why do this when we have tried and true formulas that worked for centuries, and all we have to do to find them is do a little research? The same is true of the gods. We could try to get to know them through prayer and rites alone, and this is a good part of Heathenry, but it is easier to form a basis of who the gods are by seeing how the ancient Anglo-Saxon pagans viewed them.

There are areas of Anglo-Saxon paganism where reconstruction of the ancient Anglo-Saxon religion is not enough. In such cases, we find that we can borrow from the ancient Norse religion (the religion of the Vikings), which is closely related. Even then we may find holes in our belief system. In such cases, we may rely on Unsubstantiated Personal Gnosis or UPG for short. UPG is the idea that one's personal spiritual insights are as valid as those found through careful research into the lore (the lore being the body of texts describing the beliefs of the ancient Germanic peoples). UPG is generally frowned upon in Anglo-Saxon Heathenry, as it has little to no basis in ancient practice and belief. Yet, all Anglo-Saxon beliefs and practices, even ancient ones, probably started out as UPG. And sometimes UPG is necessary to fill out one's beliefs. Most feel however, that when talking about one's beliefs, it is important to state whether this is a belief taken from the lore, or one that is UPG. Some UPGs become common Heathen belief never the less. A good example of this is the idea Fríge (Frigga) spins the threads used by the Wyrdæ (the fates) in weaving. Nowhere in the lore is this stated, yet several Heathens have separately arrived at that conclusion. Just remember, if you have a belief that you cannot confirm as an ancient belief to tell folks it is your own opinion.

As said above, Anglo-Saxon paganism is a polytheistic religion. You may already be familiar with many of the gods that Anglo-Saxon pagans worship. Many of the day names are named for Anglo-Saxon pagan gods. Tuesday is named for the Anglo-Saxon god Tiw. Wednesday is named for the Anglo-Saxon god Wóden (pronounced Wod-en). Thursday is named for the Anglo-Saxon god Þunor (pronounced Thun-or). And Friday is named for the Anglo-Saxon goddess Fríge (pronounced Free-ya). If you are not familiar with them by these names, perhaps you know them by their Anglicized Norse names. Wóden is known as Odin in the Norse mythology. Tiw is known as Tyr in the Norse mythology. Þunor is Thor, and Fríge is Frigga in the Norse mythology. You are also familiar with the name of another Anglo-Saxon goddess though you may not even know it. Easter is named for the Anglo-Saxon goddess Éostre (pronounced ay-o-st-re).

There are many other Anglo-Saxon gods and goddesses.

Anglo-Saxon paganism is an othopraxic religion, not an orthodox one. That is it has common practices, but not a common doctrine. An orthopraxic religion is one that focuses on the transmission of tradition, ethical systems, and sacrificial offerings. An orthodox religion focuses on codified beliefs, creeds, and correct belief. Anglo-Saxon paganism has no set of codified beliefs and practices. Every individual Anglo-Saxon pagan is free to believe as they see fit. They do not have to ascribe to a set of beliefs set down by a church. There is no creed an Anglo-Saxon pagan has to live by. There is nothing like the Christian Apostle's Creed, or even the Wiccan Rede. Nowhere is there set down in writing how an Anglo-Saxon pagan should believe. Never the less, Anglo-Saxon pagans have an ethical system in common with other Anglo-Saxon pagans, and many traditions and rites as well. This is what makes it an orthopraxic religion and not an orthodox one. Because of this how Anglo-Saxon paganism is practiced may vary a great deal amongst Anglo-Saxon pagans. How the gods are seen is likely to vary as well. Many Anglo-Saxon pagans may see Þunor as merely a god of thunder, while others may see him in addition to that as a god of deep thinking. Others may see Wóden as the god of war, while others may see that as the realm of Tiw. Even how Anglo-Saxon pagans do rites may differ. Some may simply speak impromptu prayers from the heart to the gods in ritual, while others may plan elaborate memorized prayers with many layers of meaning. What virtues one emphasizes will vary too amongst Anglo-Saxon pagans. Some may hold generosity to be the highest virtue, still others hospitality, while others may give them equal weight. There is no one set way of practicing Anglo-Saxon Heathenry.

Anglo-Saxon paganism owes a lot to its related religion Asatru. Almost none of the Anglo-Saxon myths survived. But they did amongst the Norse (the Germanic people the Vikings were a part of) in two Icelandic works called the Eddas. In addition, there are many Icelandic tales called sagas that give information on the ancient Norse religion. How much of this information a modern Anglo-Saxon pagan uses is largely up to the individual. Many Anglo-Saxon pagans incorporate many Asatru practices and beliefs into their worship and beliefs, while other Anglo-Saxon pagans incorporate almost none.

Who were the Anglo-Saxons?

Anglo-Saxon is a collective name for all of the Germanic tribes that invaded what is now England in the later half of the 5th century. If you are of English descent, you are descended from the Anglo-Saxons. If you speak English, you speak a language that is in a large part descended from the language of the Anglo-Saxons. The three main tribes that invaded Great Britain were known as the Angles, the Saxons, and the Jutes. However, there were other tribes that came over as well. A Germanic tribe was a tribe that spoke a Germanic language. Modern Germanic languages include English, Dutch, Danish, Norwegian, Swedish, High German, and Low German among others. All these languages evolved from what is known as Proto-Germanic, a language for which there is no written record, but is known through reconstruction by scholars. Proto-Germanic had evolved from Proto-Indo-European, and the language of the Northern Megalith Builders. Scholars only know Proto-Indo-European through reconstruction as well. Modern Indo-European languages include the above Germanic languages as well as Welsh, French, Italian, Hindi, Spanish, Armenian, Polish, Albanian, and many others (there are over a hundred Indo-European languages). All of them descend from Proto-Indo-European. Scholars reconstruct languages by comparing the words of the languages that descended from it, and then figuring out the sound shifts or changes they had to go through to be different. Sound changes in a language tend to be uniform, and follow certain laws. Once scholars learned what these sound changes were, and the laws that they operated under, they could reconstruct Proto-Germanic for example. An asterisk before a word means it is a reconstructed word, for example *wéohian.

Before coming to England, the Angles, Saxons, and Jutes lived on the continent of Europe in what is now southern Denmark and northern Germany. The Angles lived in what is now Schleswig-Holstein. The Jutes may have lived either in what is now Jutland or on the Rhine (scholars are unsure of the exact location). And the Saxons lived in what is now Northern Germany. They were not the only tribes to invade what is now England, but were the primary ones. Other tribes that came to Great Britain were the Varni, neighbors of the Angles, and the Geats of Sweden, as well as the Frisians. The Frisians came from what are now the Netherlands, and the islands off the coast of it. Prior to the invasion, there were Germanic tribes already living in what is now England. They were serving as mercenaries for the Romans. Some Saxons, Frisians, and part of a tribe known as the Alemanni were already in Great Britain prior to the invasion.

The invasion of Great Britain started around 450 CE when the Jutes established a kingdom in what is now Kent. The "Anglo-Saxon Chronicle," a record of every year of the Anglo-Saxon kingdoms, preserved how this came to pass.

> In their days Hengest and Horsa, invited by Wurtgern, king of the Britons, landed in Britain in a place that is called Ipwines fleet; first of all to support the Britons, but they afterwards fought against them. The king directed them to fight against the Picts; and they did so; and obtained the victory wheresoever they came. They then sent to the Angles, and desired them to send more assistance. They described the worthlessness of the Britons, and the richness of the land. They then sent them greater support. Then came the men from three powers of Germany; the Old Saxons, the Angles, and the Jutes. (James Ingram, translator, Everyman Press, London, 1912)

The Christian monk Bede writing in his "Ecclesiastical History" gives a slightly different account:

> They consulted what was to be done, and where they should seek assistance to prevent or repel the cruel and frequent incursions of the northern nations; and

they all agreed with their King Vortigern to call over to their aid, from the parts beyond the sea, the Saxon nation; which, as the event still more evidently showed, appears to have been done by the appointment of our Lord Himself, that evil might fall upon them for their wicked deeds.

Bede goes onto say:

IN the year of our Lord 449, Martian being made emperor with Valentinian, and the forty-sixth from Augustus, ruled the empire seven years. Then the nation of the Angles, or Saxons, being invited by the aforesaid king, arrived in Britain with three longships, and had a place assigned them to reside in by the same king, in the eastern part of the island, that they might thus appear to be fighting for their country, whilst their real intentions were to enslave it. Accordingly they engaged with the enemy, who were come from the north to give battle, and obtained the victory; which, being known at home in their own country, as also the fertility of the country, and the cowardice of the Britons, a more considerable fleet was quickly sent over, bringing a still greater number of men, which, being added to the former, made up an invincible army. The newcomers received of the Britons a place to inhabit, upon condition that they should wage war against their enemies for the peace and security of the country, whilst the Britons agreed to furnish them with pay. Those who came over were of the three most powerful nations of Germany Saxons, Angles, and Jutes. From the Jutes are descended the people of Kent, and of the Isle of Wight, and those also in the province of the West Saxons who are to this day called Jutes, seated opposite to the Isle of Wight. From the Saxons, that is, the country which is now called Old Saxony, came the East Saxons, the South Saxons, and the West Saxons. From the Angles, that is, the country which is called

Anglia, and which is said, from that time, to remain desert to this day, between the provinces of the Jutes and the Saxons, are descended the East Angles, the Midland Angles, Mercians, all the race of the Northumbrians, that is, of those nations that dwell on the north side of the river Humber, and the other nations of the English. (translator unknown, E.P. Dutton, New York, 1910)

The religions of these tribes were related to the religion of the ancient Vikings, another Germanic people. You have already read the names of some of their gods and goddesses. They worshiped in groves and temples. They held sacred feasts, and paid homage to ancestors in song and in poem. Their lives revolved around working the fields, waging war when needed, celebrating the changes of the year, and worshiping their gods. Everything was dictated by customs and traditions. They had no need of books to teach them what to do, but instead relied on the spoken word. These words often took the form of poems for easy memorization.

Once in Great Britain, the tribes quickly began to establish kingdoms. In all, seven kingdoms comprised what is now known as the Heptarchy. Amongst the seven kingdoms that comprised the Heptarchy were Kent, which was formed by the Jutes; Merica, East Anglia, and Northumbria, which were formed by the Angles; and Essex, Sussex, and Wessex, which were formed by the Saxons. There were many smaller kingdoms as well including the Isle of Wight, Lindsey, Surrey, and the Middle Angles, as well as others.

The Anglo-Saxons were left to practice their brand of paganism for about 150 years. Then in 593 CE, Pope Gregory sent Augustine as a missionary to the Germanic tribes in Great Britain. Augustine arrived in 597 CE on the Isle of Thanet, and began preaching to the Anglo-Saxon pagans. By 601 CE he convinced King Eðelbert of Kent whose wife was a Christian Frank (the Franks were another Germanic tribe and ancestors to the modern French) to outlaw Heathenry and convert to Christianity. Thus, the end of Anglo-Saxon paganism had started. Over the next fifty or so years, kingdoms would convert to Christianity and then convert back to Heathenry. Sometimes, a Christian king would convert a kingdom; only to be overthrown and have the kingdom converted back. Other times a king's son upon succession would convert the kingdom back to Heathenry. Overall though, the trend was towards kings and thus their kingdoms becoming Christian.

Finally, King Penda of Mercia (an Anglo-Saxon kingdom in the midlands of England) made the last stand of Anglo-Saxon paganism. His career began in 628 CE when he fought and defeated the West Saxons near Cirencester. For the next twenty-seven years he would fight and defeat Christian king after Christian king. One thing needs to be made clear though, Penda did not fight the Christian kings because he was anti-Christian. Indeed, he allowed many in his kingdom to convert to Christianity, including his own son Peada. Penda could not tolerate hypocrites though. Bede, the Christian monk wrote that Penda said, "They were contemptible and wretched who did not obey their God, in whom they believed." In 633 CE, we are told Penda became king of the Mercians, and that year he defeated Edwin of Northumbria (an Anglo-Saxon kingdom on the northeast coast of England), a king that had converted to Christianity a few years before. Between 633 and 646 CE, Penda tried to keep East Anglia under his subjugation killing kings Sigebert, Egric, and Anna in battle. He then turned his sights on Northumbria again, and on August 5, 642 CE he fought Oswald of Northumbria. He again won the battle. Penda then drove Cenwalh of Wessex from his kingdom for having put his sister away in 645 CE. There were no doubts numerous battles that were not recorded. Every single battle recorded though with the exception of one, Penda won. On November 15, 655 CE (or possibly 654 CE) came Penda's final battle, the battle of Winwaed. It is thought by scholars to have taken place near what is now Leeds. According to Bede, Penda took with him 30 legions to attack King Oswiu of Northumbria, so the army must have been immense. Penda's guide into the area was Oswiu's own nephew, Æðelwold, king of Deira (a kingdom that formed part of Northumbria). The river Winwaed was flooded, and Penda had several troops desert. Cadafael ap Cynfeddw of Gwynedd fled with his troops the night before the battle took place. And Æðelwold retreated shortly before the battle began. By the end of the day, Penda laid dead, his army scattered. Thus died the last great Anglo-Saxon pagan king, descendant of the god Wóden himself (ten generations removed), and the man that had turned Mercia from being a vassal state of Northumbria into the greatest power in all England. There were Anglo-Saxon pagan kings after Penda, but none with his power. In 685 CE, Cadwalla took the throne of Wessex to become the last Anglo-Saxon Heathen king. In 686, the Isle of Wight, the last truly Anglo-Saxon pagan stronghold was converted to Christianity, and King Cadwalla of Wessex converted to Christianity in 688 CE. By that time, all Anglo-Saxon kings were Christian, and much of the populace. England would not see Heathen kings again until the Danes invaded in the ninth century.

    The Anglo-Saxons left a definite mark on the history of English-speaking peoples. We owe much of our form of government to them, and many of our laws as well. Our culture is full of their customs and traditions. Some of our holidays such as Easter date back to when Heathen gods were worshiped instead of the Christian one. Our language owes much of its lexicon to Old English. Our most common words such as "the," "me," "you," "house," "horse," "sister," "brother," "father," "mother," all come from Old English. Many of the virtues we hold dear date back to when the ancient Anglo-Saxons were alive. A strong work ethic, the ideas of giving to others, welcoming folks into our homes were all things that the ancient Anglo-Saxons held dear. Without the Anglo-Saxons many of you would not be sitting here, and if you were, you would not be reading and speaking in English. It is sad that we are not often taught about them in our schools as children. After all, as stated before, were it not for them, many of us would not be sitting here.

Gods, Goddesses, and Other Beings

What is a God?

A god is a very powerful spirit that helps Mankind in some way. They differ from other spirits in that they gave gifts to Man to make him a spiritual being, and continue to seek to help him. In the Anglo-Saxon pantheon there are two families of gods, the Ése (pronounced ees-uh) called the Æsir in the Norse myths, and the Wen called the Vanir in the Norse myths. There are also a variety of other deities not of these families such as Éostre and Hreda. There are many powerful beings that are not gods, in that they do not help Mankind, and in some cases seek to hurt Man, and these are best avoided. There are also a variety of lesser beings that may sometimes help Mankind such as the elves and dwarves, not to mention the house wights (a wight is any spirit and is pronounced "white") that take care of the home.

Anglo-Saxon pagans seek to develop a relationship with their gods and goddesses. This is done through prayer and ritual. When you first start trying to reach out to the gods and goddesses, pick one out that appeals to you. Then just talk to them, as you would your friend. Do not expect a response. The gods and goddesses are not ones to speak necessarily, but they are great listeners. You may want to make a small offering of mead (honey wine), wine, or food. If you are underage, juice or milk can be substituted for the mead or wine. When giving such gifts to the gods and goddesses, find, if you can a quiet place in nature, and simply tell them you are giving this gift to them. If you have no such place available to you, find a public park or other such place (leaving food out in public parks probably violates some laws, and you may not be permitted alcohol in them, but you can certainly pour out some juice or milk). Once you have given your gift to the god or goddess you have chosen to speak to, speak to them from your heart. Let them know what is on your mind. If you are having problems in school or at work, let them know about the problems, and ask for their help. It is best to ask help of gods and goddesses you have worked with in the past. A god or goddess you have not developed a relationship with is unlikely to help you. If you are just starting out, make a few offerings before you ask for anything. To do so otherwise would be sort of like meeting a stranger on the street, giving them a gift, and then asking for a favor. It is important that you make offerings each time you ask for help with anything. The gods and goddesses do not necessarily help someone for nothing.

While you may ask the gods and goddesses for help, they are not your best friend, big brother, big sister, father, mother, grandfather, grandmother, or even kindly uncle or aunt. It is important to remember they are very powerful beings that help us because we give gifts to them. Some folks think they can develop very personal relationships with the gods and goddesses. This is highly unlikely. There are thousands of Heathens, and were the gods and goddesses to dedicate time to each one daily, they would never get anything else done. Many feel that we are descended from the gods and goddesses, and if we look at the lore, we will find this is true. According to a medieval Scandinavian work, the "Heimskringla" the Swedish kings are descended from the god Yngvi-Freyr (our Anglo-Saxon god Ing). The Anglo-Saxon kings' lists show Wóden and Seaxnéat as the ancestor of many of the Anglo-Saxon kings. And we are all descended from Mannus and his sons according to the Roman work "Germania." We have the blood of gods running through us, and for that reason the gods and goddesses have a vested interest in us. However, it is important we never take them for granted. "A gift always calls for a gain," says the Elder Edda (an Icelandic work compiled in the Middle Ages and containing tales of the Norse gods, gnomic wisdom, and tales of heroes), and this is the way it is with the gods. If we want something of them, we must give gifts to them. They will not help us simply because we are descended from them. Think of it this way, if your brother always forgot your birthday, would you be likely to get him a birthday gift? Perhaps you would, but many would not. It is no different with the gods. If you are always asking for something, but never giving anything in return, why should they help you?

In addition to always giving gifts to the gods when asking something of them, you must always be respectful of them. The ancient Heathens often knelt before their idols. In "Flateyjarbók" (one of the Icelandic sagas) Hakon falls prostrate before the goddess Þórgerðr. A similar scene is seen in "Hörd's Saga" (another Icelandic saga) where Þórstein falls before an idol and speaks to it. Such scenes are common throughout the lore. The ancient Germanic Heathens held deep respect for their gods, and revered them in such a way that showed that respect. While I am not suggesting you fall prostrate before your idols, I am saying you should approach them with deep respect.

What follows are descriptions of the major Anglo-Saxon gods and goddesses, followed by a bit on the wights or spirits such as the elves and dwarves. In parenthesizes after the Anglo-Saxon god name is the Norse.

Wóden

Wóden (Odin) is king of the Ése, and considered foremost amongst the gods. His name derives from Proto-Germanic *wod-eno- which means "raging, mad, inspired." His name probably comes from his position as leader of the Wild Hunt. The Wild Hunt is a group of phantasmal, spectral huntsmen that fly though the air on winter storms hunting at night collecting the souls of the wayward and lost. They are made up of the dead souls of wermen (males) and women. Wóden's frenzy can also be seen in the Norse lore when one examines tales of the berserkers, warriors dedicated to Wóden that would go into a battle frenzy, killing all that got into their path. According to our earliest records, he is a battle god. As early as Tacitus' "Germania" we see him as accepting the spoils of war as sacrifices.

Wóden is no mere mad man intent on battle though. He is also the god of poetry and speech. The Eddas speak of how Wóden won Óðroerir (pronounced oath-roarer) "the mead of inspiration" which allows poets to compose great poetry; how he won the runes; and gave man the gift of "divine breath." The "Anglo-Saxon Rune Poem" credits Wóden with being the origin of all speech. As god of poetry, Wóden was also god of galdor, "magical incantation." In the Eddas, Wóden is shown to have won the runes for Man and the gods. In the "Nine Worts Galdor" (an Anglo-Saxon magical charm), he is said to have gifted Man with nine healing herbs. Indeed, Wóden is seen as a god of healing. In addition to the "Nine Worts Galdor," there is the "Second Merseberg Charm" (a German magical charm) in which he is seen healing an injured horse. Perhaps linked to his being god of poetry and speech, Wóden also is constantly seeking wisdom. We are told in the Eddas, that he gave one of his eyes to Mimer's Well to gain wisdom. In the "Anglo-Saxon Rune Poem," not only are we told that he is the origin of all speech, but that speech is "wisdom's support and the wise man's help."

Wóden is also god of kings. All of the kings of the Anglo-Saxon kingdoms, save one, are said to be descended from Wóden. This is perhaps because of his position as king of the gods. Wóden is thought by scholars to be the god referred to by Roman chroniclers as Mercury. Mercury amongst his many duties is also the guide to dead souls in the Roman mythology. This has lead many to believe that Wóden must fill the same role.

Wóden is a complex deity, one with many facets to him. He is not one to be followed lightly. He keeps people to what they have agreed to, no matter what the cost. Many have pledged their service to him only to regret it later. For that reason, if you feel drawn to Wóden you should consider long and hard about whether you want to dedicate yourself to him. Having Wóden as a patron is a difficult path. Therefore, dedicating yourself to him is not something that should be taken lightly. If you feel you should dedicate yourself to Wóden, then it is advised that you also dedicate yourself to Fríge, his wife, as well. Fríge helps moderate how Wóden treats his adherents. In several places in the lore, she is seen, often tricking Wóden into doing the right thing. It took years before I learned this, but once I did my life was made a whole lot easier.

Fríge

Fríge (Frigga) is queen of the Ése. She is the most powerful of the goddess. Her primary domain is that of the household. However, do not let this mislead you. A woman in ancient Germanic society was the head of the household, often making the most vital decisions concerning it. A woman of that time bore all the keys to the house, including that of the household treasures. Like Wóden, she has great wisdom. She is said to know the future of all things. She never speaks these things though. In the myth of the origin of the Lombards, she is said to have tricked Wóden. The then Winni, as the Lombards were then called, were at war with the Vandals, and about to enter into battle with them. The Vandals made sacrifices to Wóden for victory in battle, and he granted it to them. The Winni then made offerings to Fríge, not knowing what else to do. So Fríge told the Winni to have their women stand with the wermen with their hair over their faces the day of the battle. She then turned Wóden's bed so it faced the Winni. When Wóden awoke, he said, "Who are these long beards?" Fríge then told him, "Now you have named them, you must give them victory." The Winni became the Lombards and won the battle.

Fríge is the goddess of mothers and children, and according to the Icelandic sagas was called upon in birth of a child. Fríge is also associated with spinning, and the belt of the constellation of Orion was once called Frigga's Distaff. As queen of Ésageard (Asgard, home of the Ése), she has the duties of any nobleman's wife. This means she advises Wóden as well as plays the role of peacemaker, often intervening to make and maintain peace. Fríge is a very important goddess in the elimination of strife.

People that run their family's household, or their own are wise to invoke Fríge often. Mothers and fathers especially should develop a relationship with her to help with their children. It is advisable if you are dedicated to Wóden to also dedicate yourself to Fríge as well.

Þunor

Þunor (Thor) is one of the Ése. In ancient times, Þunor was the god of the common man, at least amongst the Norse. There is no reason to doubt that the Anglo-Saxons were any different. Þunor is the god of thunder, and as such governs storms and rains. As god of the rains, he also is a fertility god, and he and his wife Sibb (Sif) are often thanked at the holy tide Hláfmæst for the wheat crop of the year. But he is no mere thunder god. Þunor is invoked to hallow areas and items for sacred use. One of his nicknames amongst the Norse means "the hallower" for that reason.

Þunor is a god of raw strength, and he uses this strength to fight the giants that would harm Man and the gods. He is therefore seen as the defender of Mankind. His hammer that he uses for this purpose is often duplicated as pendants that adherents of Heathenry wear. They are thought to offer protection as well as mark one as Heathen so all will know.

Þunor is also god of the thing, or tribal assembly. In Iceland, assemblies were always held on Thursday for this reason. He is one of three gods that oaths were sworn by (the other two being Wóden and Ing. The Norse called þunor "the deep thinker", and perhaps it is because of his deep thought that he was seen as the god of assemblies amongst them.

Of all the gods, Þunor is the one nearly everyone seems to make offerings to. He is by far perhaps one of the most popular gods in modern Anglo-Saxon paganism. Only Wóden seems to garner more attention. Þunor seems to be the most approachable of the gods, and for that reason perhaps he is a good god for those new to Anglo-Saxon paganism to approach. With humans, he is an easygoing deity that does not make many demands. Yet, he has so much to offer in return. Those working especially in farming, or blue-collar jobs would do good to make offerings to him.

Tiw

Tiw (Tyr) is one of the Ése. Tiw is the war god, more than that; he is the god of victory. In the "Elder Edda" we are told to scratch the rune named for him into weapons. Tiw is also known for his bravery. In the "Prose Edda" we are told how he agreed to put his hand in the mouth of the giant wolf Fenris in order that the wolf be bound. Tiw did so, and lost his hand as a result. With this act, he displayed a whole host of virtues that embody the heroic idea. Bravery, the importance of keeping one's word is one he shown, not to mention that he did it to protect the community of gods from the wolf. Indeed, Tiw is the deity of the heroic idea. We are told in the "Anglo-Saxon Rune Poem:"

> Tiw is a token --- who holds troth well with princes --- he is ever on course over night's mists --- he never betrays.

Like Þunor, Tiw was seen as god of the assembly by the ancient Germanic peoples. Germanic mercenaries erected an altar on Hadrian's Wall to Mars Thingus, "Mars of the Thing." The Old High German name for Tuesday "Tiw's Day" is Dienstag "Assembly Day."

Tiw is a good deity to follow if you are a soldier or law enforcement officer. Lawyers, judges, and other folks involved in the arbitration of law would do well to follow him as well. Tiw, while not as approachable as Þunor, is still not a difficult god to create a relationship with. Those seeking justice would do well to make offerings to him.

Ing

Ing (Yngvi Freyr) is one of the Wen. He is sometimes called Fréa (pronounced Fra-uh where the a is like that in at). The evidence for a god Ing is sporadic at best like with so many of the Anglo-Saxon deities. What information we have is far from conclusive especially when considering whether Ing and Freyr are the same deity. The earliest hint of the deity is in Pliny's *Natural History* (IV.99). Here he lists as one of five confederations of Germanic tribes the Ingvaeones. The name Ingvaeones is thought to mean "friends of Ing." Tacitus in his work "Germania" takes it one step farther giving us a bit of myth to go with the name:

> In their ancient songs, their only way of remembering or recording the past they celebrate an earth-born god Tuisco, and his son Mannus, as the origin of their race, as their founders. To Mannus they assign three sons, from whose names, they say, the coast tribes are called Ingaevones; those of the interior, Herminones; all the rest, Istaevones.

This myth parallels one in Hindu myth, Manu is said to have had two sons and three daughters, and to have been the ancestor of all mankind. One myth attributed to him is saving Mankind from a great flood. He is seen as the first king in the history of Mankind. The similarity is uncanny, and seems to indicate a common Indo-European origin for a god named Man.

The tale in "Germania" is not the only shell of a myth in regards to Ing. He is also mentioned in the Anglo-Saxon Rune Poem, his name being the name of one of the runes:

> Ing was first – among the East Danes
> Seen by men – but he since went eft (back)
> Over the wet way – his wain (wagon) ran after
> Thus the Heardings – named the hero

Here Ing is listed as a hero and not a deity. However, this may be a change created by a Christian scribe and not lore per se. Too, it could be as a tribal ancestor he is thought to be a hero as well as a deity. Ing is also potentially named in the kings' list of Bernicia where an Ingui is listed. It is possible that like Wóden for the Mercian line he was seen as ancestor of the entire line before later additions.

The Swedes called Ing, Yngvi Freyr, and their kings were thought to descend from him. Here we are faced with a controversy, was Ing and Freyr seen as the same deity. In favor of this is the procession in a wagon, as well as the name, and both are seen as ancestor deities. Against the two being one and the same are the differing fathers, Njord for Freyr and Mannus for Ing. It is possible that Mannus and Njord are one and the same. But then there is also the possibility that Njord was not considered Freyr's father until late in Heathen Era. There is probably no real solution to the problem unless new evidence comes to light (such as a Norse poem listing Mannus as Freyr's father).

Ing is above all else a fertility deity. He is to be invoked when one is seeking to grow things in the garden or fields. He is also a god of prosperity as well as of peace. His title Fréa is related to words meaning "peace." His symbol is the boar, and images of boars were thought by the ancient Germanic peoples to offer protection in battle.

Ing is a very approachable deity. He is easy to follow and makes few demands. In the Icelandic lore some of his followers are portrayed and they always seem to be living healthy, productive lives.

Fréo

Fréo (pronounced Fra-o where the a is like that in at) is one of the Wen. Fréo is Ing's sister. She is called Freya amongst those in Asatru. Some feel she and Fríge are one and the same goddess. This is mainly because Fréo does not appear anywhere in the Old English literature, and finding place name evidence for her is difficult as her name so resembles the title of Ing, Fréa. However, in the Norse literature, her and Fríge appear as separate goddesses. They would also seem to govern different domains.

Fréo is a goddess of magic. She is said to have taught Wóden a form of magic usually only practiced by women in the Eddas. She also governs human sexuality, and according to the Icelandic sagas she was invoked along with Fríge when people got married. She is also a war goddess. Half those killed in battle go to her hall (the other half go to Wóden).

Fréo should be invoked in matters of love, and especially at weddings. People seeking to have children would do well to pray to her often. She does not seem to be a difficult goddess to follow, and seems kind to her followers.

Hama

Hama (Heimdall) is one of the Ése. He is watchman of the gods, keeping guard over the rainbow bridge that leads to Ésageard (home of the gods). In the Eddas he is called the "white god," and this could be due to his purity. He seems to have some link to Fréo. In the Norse lore he is said to have done battle with Loki (the Norse trickster figure) over the necklace Brosingamene. In "Beowulf (an Old English epic poem)" he is represented as a hero stealing back the same necklace. Brosingamene is a necklace owned by Fréo. Finally, his Norse name Heimdall corresponds with a Norse name of Fréo's, Mardoll.

I have never worked with Hama personally. But he always gave me the impression of being a very protective deity, and one that could be counted on.

Neorð

Neorð (Njord) is one of the Wen. He is listed as Ing's father in the Norse lore. He is the god of commerce, especially sea commerce. It is said in the Eddas and Icelandic sagas that sailors and fisherman alike for good seas invoked him. He is therefore seen as a god of prosperity much like Ing. Never the less, he does not appear in the Old English literature.

Neorð is an approachable deity, and should be made offerings to by those that live by the sea.

Neorðu

Neorðu (Nerthus) is mentioned by the Roman Tacticus in his work "Germania." He had the following to say:

> After the Langobardi come the Reudigni, Auiones, Angli, Varni, Eudoses, Suarines and Nuithones all well guarded by rivers and forests. There is nothing remarkable about any of these tribes unless it be the common worship of Nerthus, that is Earth Mother. They believe she is interested in men's affairs and drives among them. On an island in the ocean sea there is a sacred grove wherein waits a holy wagon covered by a drape. One priest only is allowed to touch it. He can feel the presence of the goddess when she is there in her sanctuary and accompanies her with great reverence as she is pulled along by kine. It is a time of

festive holidaymaking in whatever place she decides to honour with her advent and stay. No one goes to war, no one takes up arms, in fact every weapon is put away, only at that time are peace and quiet known and prized until the goddess, having had enough of people's company, is at last restored by the same priest to her temple. After which the wagon and the drape, and if you like to believe me, the deity herself is bathed in a mysterious pool. The rite is performed by slaves who, as soon as it is done, are drowned in the lake. In this way mystery begets dread and a pious ignorance concerning what that sight may be which only those who are about to die are allowed to see. (Germania, ch. 40).

This is the only information we have on the goddess. We do know however, that her procession bears similarities to later ones told of the god Ing, and that her name is a feminine version of the god Neorð. Like Ing's temples in which weapons were banned, all weapons were put away during her procession. Tacitus tells us that she is the Tellus Mater or "Earth Mother," and many have taken this to mean she was the Earth Goddess. In all probability she was not the Earth Mother, but instead was the Earth goddess of the Wen. Some feel is the sister and consort of Neorð, Snorri having said in the *Ynglinga Saga* (an Icelandic history of the Swedish kings) that brother sister marriage were customary amongst the Vanir. She was certainly known to the ancient Angles, whether the other Anglo-Saxon pagan tribes worshiped her is not known.

Ėostre

Ėostre is only known because the Christian monk Bede mentioned her in his "De Temporum Ratione (The

Reckoning of Time) where he spoke of a month named in her honor. Despite this lack of information, we have many traditions associated with her holy tide that survived due their being absorbed into the Christian holiday of Easter (which takes its name from hers). Ėostre would therefore appear to be a goddess of fertility, hares and eggs being associated with her. Her name is also related to that of Greek goddess Eos, goddess of the dawn in their pantheon. It could be that Ėostre is goddess of the dawn, or due to when the month named for her took place, a goddess of the spring. According to Jakob Grimm in his work "Teutonic Mythology" dew or water collected from streams on Easter day was thought especially holy. Beautiful maidens in sheer white were said to seen frolicking in the countryside. Also according to Grimm, the white maiden of Osterrode, was said to appear with a large batch of keys at her belt, and stride to the brook to collect water on Easter morning. Ėostre would therefore also seem to be a goddess of purity as well as perhaps the dawn and spring.

Ėostre is a very easy going goddess, and a very giving one. She seems always grateful for offerings. Like her holy tide, offering should always be done with a great deal of joy, and light heartedness.

Hreda

Hreda is an Anglo-Saxon goddess mentioned by Bede in "De Temporum Ratione" for whom Hreðmonað (roughly March) was named for. Some derive her name from Old English hréð "glory, fame, triumph, honor," which is cognate to Old High German hruod and Old Norse hroðr, both of which mean glorious. It was Grimm that first put forth a possible connection to Old High German hruod and Old Norse hroðr. The scholar Phillip Shaw put forth the theory her name came from Old English hræd "swift." Hræd is hred in the Mercian and Kentish dialects of Old English. And others derive her name from hréðe "cruel." Figuring out which word her name derives from is complicated by the fact

Bede used "d" for both "d" and "ð." With so many theories as to what word her name is derived from it is difficult to formulate anything about her. Brian Smith, Alderman of White Marsh Theod believes her to be a winter goddess. He ascribes to the idea her name is derived from hréðe "cruel," and relates this to the fickleness of late winter when it can be sunny and warm one day and snowing and frigid cold the next. Still others believe she is a warrior goddess drawing on hréð "glory, fame, triumph, honor." It would be difficult to arrive at any conclusions. It is perhaps only through her worship we will ever know anything about her.

In my offerings to Hreda, I have found her to be very grateful for anything given her. My offerings to her have been some of the most fulfilling I have ever made. She therefore should not be ignored simply because of a lack of information on her. It is only through her worship we will learn her nature.

Seaxnéat

Seaxnéat is only mentioned in two sources. One is a renunciation formula that had to be performed by the Saxons before baptism where he is listed with Wóden and Þunor. The other is in the genealogies of the kings of Essex. Scholars because of this have often linked him to Tiw, assuming he must have been an important deity to be placed beside two of the greater deities. A few have argued that he may be Ing. His name means "sword friend."

I have never worked with Seaxnéat, other than making a couple of offerings. I suspect though, due to his name, he might be a good deity for soldiers to invoke when going into combat.

Helið

Helið is a god or goddess mentioned in a few late

sources and associated with the Cerne Abbey. The earliest of these sources is a tale about Augustine destroying her idol by William of Coventry. Located at the abbey is a holy spring, which may have been there in the day of her worship there. John Leland writing in the sixteenth century called Helið the "Saxon Esculapius, or preserver of health." The fact the names do resemble known Middle and Early Modern English words for health also adds some credence to this possibility this god or goddess existed as an Anglo-Saxon pagan deity.

I feel Helið is probably a goddess. I get this impression when praying to her for healing of others and myself. She seems to be an easygoing goddess, rather care free, but serious when it comes time to making someone better.

The Ancestors

One's ancestors are especially revered in Anglo-Saxon paganism. Indeed, many call on them for help before they would any of the gods or goddesses. This is because our ancestors have a vested interest in us. Just as we want to see our children be successful, so too, do the ancestors want to see their descendants be successful. Ancestors are in many ways like the guardian angels of Christianity. They watch over us and try to keep us safe. Our ancient ancestors respected their ancestors. This began as soon as they had passed from the realm of Middangeard (the plane we live on) to the great beyond with the funeral. The epic Old English poem "Beowulf" gives us an image of what a Heathen funeral may have been like. Beowulf was cremated. This started with the building of the pyre, and the burning of the body with all the grave goods. As the fire burned, the folk mourned. This mourning probably consisted of dirges, wailing, and what we think typical of mourning. After the body was burned, a mound was built to contain the ashes. More grave goods were added, and the mound enclosed. Once the mound was complete, 12 warriors rode around it chanting a dirge, and songs of praise for Beowulf.

This was probably typical of the funerals of the age, and gives us some idea of the respect they gave the newly dead. The songs of praise no doubt would be sung again and again at symbels (ritual drinking rounds, symbel will be covered in a later chapter) in years to come, and thus keep the memory of the deceased alive. The next event in regards to the newly dead was the erfi as it was called in Old Norse (reconstructed as *ierfealu in Old English). This was a round of ritual toasts especially dedicated to the recently deceased person done several months after the funeral. At it, the heirs received their inheritance, and the new ancestor was praised in the minni (a memory toast) as it was called in Old Norse done by their direct heir after he or she took the High Seat.

Archaeologists have found evidence of the burning of grain in Anglo-Saxon graveyards, such as at Portway in Hampshire, England, and this is attested to by the 7th century Penitentials of Theodore, which forbade burning grain for the well being of the dead. In addition to this activity of gifting grain to the dead, they were remembered in symbel (symbel will be covered in the chapter on rites). In symbel, as part of the gielp (boast of one's past deeds) one gave their parentage or ancestry, and this can be seen as an act of respect for the ancestors. Children were named for ancestors, and it was thought they inherited their ancestor's luck. There is plenty of evidence of a deep respect for the ancestors in the lore, and more than enough for a basis of practice today.

Of particular importance to the ancient Heathen were the Idesa (called the Dísir in Old Norse). There is much evidence for the worship of the tribal mothers in the lore. Germanic mercenaries in the Roman legions made altars to the Matronae, or "Mothers" along Hadrian's Wall in England, and others on the continent. These altars were to deities with names such as Alatievia, Gabiae, and Aufanie. Scholar Rudolf Simek links the Norse Dísir to the Matronae, and also links Anglo-Saxon Modraniht, "Mothers Night" (the first night of the Anglo-Saxon pagan calendar) to the Matronae. Amongst the Norse, the Dísir were worshiped at Dísablót (a time when the ancestral mothers were offered to). According to "Víga-Glúms saga" at Winter Nights (a Norse holy tide held in October) the dísablót was performed, though the "Heimskringla" places it in February or March. These were not communal celebrations, but family gatherings, although the Dísablót mentioned in "Víga-Glúms saga" was quite large. The Dísir in the Norse lore were seen as protectors of the family, while the inscriptions to the Matronae were calls for help in time of need, requests to watch over the family or clan, requests to help in fertility and childbirth, requests to heal, as well as requests to give protection in battle.

So what does this mean for the modern Anglo-Saxon pagan? Largely, it means perhaps we should try to learn about our ancestry, and give respect to those ancestors we deem worthy. Genealogy is an excellent way of getting in touch with one's ancestors, even if one can only trace the line back a few generations. Naming children for dead ancestors is another way to get in touch with one's ancestors. Children named for an ancestor are thought to inherit some of the ancestor's luck. There are many ways we can respect our ancestors. I have burnt grain at the graves of my parents. I take a fire pot to their grave and in it place some grain. Using vodka or another sort of alcohol I set the grain alight and allow it to burn until all the grain is gone. All the while I am saying prayers to my ancestors and praising them. I also often remember them in the minni or myne (as it would be called in Old English) of symbel, and during making offerings. Usually, I say something in praise of something they have done, or simply wish them well in the afterlife. At the major feasts such as Yule, we set a plate aside for the ancestors with a little of each food present. It is then given with the offering to the gods.

I have an ancestral altar in my home with pictures of

ancestors upon it. On such a shrine, one can keep mementos of the ancestor, perhaps a grandfather's straight razor or a grandmother's embroidery. Anything that had meaning to the ancestor can be placed on the altar. One may wish to do regular rites at the altar, perhaps even daily ones. I burn incense at mine, and offer them wine on special occasions. Daily prayers would not be out of line. Indeed, the ancestors were probably worshiped more than the major Gods in ancient times.

A custom we kept in White Sage Kindred of Dallas, Texas was that every Winter Nights we would honor the ancestors of the members. We would set up a special altar to them. On it we would place pictures that the ancestors had brought with them for that purpose. The offering as well as a good part of the symbol was dedicated to them. In years to come, as Heathens pass on, ancestor worship will become even more important, as the anniversaries of Heathens' deaths will become a time to make offerings to them and remember them.

A large part of Heathenry is a deep respect for the ancestors, for their deeds, and keeping their memories alive. This is especially important to families as ancestors form a part of the family. Families are not just the living members of a family, but the dead as well.

One problem that is sometimes encountered amongst Heathens is they may not be particularly proud of their ancestors. Some come from families filled with abuse or alcoholism. In such cases, it must be remembered you have literally millions of ancestors, and not all of them can be bad. So if every ancestor you can name is a bad seed, go back further, and pray to those nameless ancestors who may have been more honorable. Another problem sometimes encountered is when someone is adopted and therefore does not know who their ancestors are. If that is the case with you, do not worry. You can always pay respect to your adoptive parents' ancestors, or you could simply call on your ancestors from your biological parents even though you do not know their names.

Many Anglo-Saxon pagans daily pray to their ancestors, and make small offerings throughout the month. Offerings are made to ancestors the same way that they are for the gods, and this will be covered in a later chapter.

Elves, Cofgodas, and Other Beings

In the Norse lore elves are associated with the gods, particularly the Ése, though there are also links to the Wen. They are portrayed as being somewhere between gods and men, and we are told offerings were made to them. They are incredibly handsome, sometimes called beautiful in the lore, and often associated with the Sun. They are also associated with the god Ing, who is said to have gotten Ælfgeard (home of the elves) as a gift for his first tooth. Snorri, author of the "Prose Edda" divides the elves into two groups; Ljosalfar or "light elves" and Dokkalfar also called the Svartálfar or "dark elves." Scholars have come to doubt this division preferring to think that the dark elves are instead dwarves. The elves were not all light and happiness in the Norse lore. Wayland (called Volundr by the Norse) was a vengeful character. Having been taken captive and forced to make jewelry and weapons for an evil king, he takes his revenge by molesting the king's daughter and killing his sons. There is little reason to doubt that the Anglo-Saxons saw elves as being any different. Indeed, there is some evidence to show they saw them much the same. Elf names such as Ælfred are common in ancient Anglo-Saxon England, and Ælf- "elf" in names and words is commonly seen associated with many of the qualities of elves in the Norse lore.

Elves were not seen as nice beings all the time though. There are several Anglo-Saxon healing charms whose purpose is to cure ailments caused by elves. Alaric Hall in his scholarly work "Elves in Anglo-Saxon England" believes that the idea that elves caused illness may be tied to an idea that the elves caused the illness to punish someone for a transgression against them. Still, elves are aligned with men and gods, as opposed to the monsters such as the thurses (a type of giant known for their destructive tendencies).

Elves therefore are a very handsome race; often described as beautiful. Indeed, Alaric Hall says some of the descriptions portray them as almost feminine. They are close in status to that of the gods. Like the gods and ancestors they accept offerings from Mankind. They tend to like natural places, and often take care of them. However, they are much like humans. They have different personalities, and some may wish to help people while others perhaps could care less. The Norse had a time when they made offerings to the elves called Álfarblót. This has carried over into modern practice in Asatru. Anglo-Saxon pagans generally do not have a specific time when they honor them instead doing it throughout the year.

There are other spirits Anglo-Saxon pagans make offerings to. Primary amongst these are the cofgodas or house wights. These are spirits that take care of your home. If offerings are made to them they can be quite helpful. Generally, oatmeal or porridge is offered to them although some Anglo-Saxon pagans offer them beer, mead, or wine as well. If not offered to, house wights are likely to hide things from you until you do make an offering. If you have things go missing around your home such as keys, lighters, or cell phones you may have unhappy house wights. You must be careful what you offer them though. There is the tale of the shoemaker and the elves (most likely house wights). The elves help make shoes until given clothing by the shoemaker and his wife. They then leave. Cofgodas have little patience for those that are lazy and do not clean their house or apartment. They only help those that help themselves. They will not clean up after someone that is dirty or untidy. However, if offered to regularly, house wights will keep your home a joyful place to live.

There are many other wights, most of whom offerings are not made to. Most of these fit in the category of monsters. One race that is helpful to gods and men are the dwarves. The dwarves live in the earth and are master smiths. In the Norse lore they are the ones that created Fréo's necklace Brosingamene. They also created Þunor's hammer, Wóden's spear, and Ing's ship. However, other places in the lore show that the dwarves are not to be trusted. In the Norse lore, Reginn causes Sigurd as much trouble as he does good.

Another race that is sometimes helpful to gods and men are the Eotenas or in modern English ettins, a type of giant. Some of the goddesses were originally ettins before they married gods. Still, the ettins are not generally made offerings to. This is because for the most part they are not to be trusted. Of course this depends on whom you classify as an ettin. Some feel Eorðe (Mother Earth) is an ettin as well as other gods and goddesses, and Eagor (Ægir) is definitely classed an ettin in the Norse lore. So there are always exceptions. Never the less, you are urged to use caution when approaching ettins.

There is another giant race that are never made offerings to. The þyrsas or thurses are a race that can be best defined as enemies of gods and men. Þunor is forever battling them trying to keep gods and men safe from their destructive powers. At no time should you make an offering to a thurse. They cannot be appeased, and while they may accept the offering, it will not sway them in the least. Indeed, by making the offering you only attract their attention and along with it their destructive powers.

There are many other creatures, some of which offerings are made to. There is the nicor or nixie, a water spirit that in ancient times was sometimes given an offering to prevent drowning. It was thought the spirits of certain rivers would take a life through drowning if an offering was not made to them at least once a year. Then there is the púca or puck. Depsite their name, they are not like the character Puck from Shakespeare. They are mischievous spirits often responsible for poltergeist activity. They can be appeased however, and may even become house wights if offerings are made to them. Then there is the mare, as in nightmare. These demons ride folks in their sleep causing intense pressure on the chest. They are never made offerings to. Finally, there is the hrisi, a type of giant that is said to be fair to look upon. They generally are not of much use to Mankind as they are of low intelligence and tend to spend their days throwing boulders at each other. Even though they are not bad per se, they generally are not given offerings due to their low intelligence and inability to help Man.

Key Concepts

Wyrd

Everyone has an orlæg (pronounced roughly or-lag) or orlay as it is called in modern English, a primal law laid down by the Wyrdæ (the Fates in Anglo-Saxon paganism) at birth and sometimes modified by the Gods. There are at least two accounts of orlay being laid down for an individual in the lore, both coming from the Norse accounts. Starkaðr is one, Helgi Hundingsbane is the other.

In Starkaðr's case, it is Þunor and Wóden that determine at least part of his orlay as an adult. According to "Gautreks saga," Starkaðr is taken to a council of the gods. There he is alternately blessed by Wóden and cursed by Þunor. Wóden gave him three lifetimes, but then Þunor said he would commit a crime for each lifetime he lived. Wóden blessed him with an abundance of riches, but Þunor cursed him to never own real estate. Wóden granted him victory always in battle. Þunor cursed him to always be badly wounded in each battle. Wóden gave him the gift of poetry, but Þunor cursed him to never remember his poems. Wóden blessed him with being loved by the nobility, but Þunor said the common people would never love him. Thus Starkaðr's orlay was made or modified by the gods Wóden and Þunor.

Helgi's laying of his orlay took place at his birth. In "Helgakviða Hundingsbana I," the Wyrdæ shape a loom in the sky, and weave the threads of his orlay. They deem that he will be the best of warriors, and most famed of princes. They also deemed that he should have land, and Neri's kinswoman. Later in "Helgakviða Hundingsbana II," Helgi states that he had to kill Sigrún's father Högni and brother Bragi to wed Sigrún, and blames this on the Norns (as the Norse called the Wyrdæ). Other Norse accounts indicate that events are determined by the Norns. In "Reginsmál," the dwarf Andvari states he was doomed to dwell in water by an evil Norn. In "Sigurðarkviða hin skamma," Brynhild blames her longing for Sigurd on the Norns. In "Guðrúnarkviða II," Atli is told by the Norns in a dream he would die at Gudrun's hands.

Looking again at Starkaðr, we begin to see a different story. We are told in Saxo's "Gesta Danorum (History of the Danes)" Starkaðr's three crimes. The first is the murder of King Vikar. According to "Gautrek's saga," Vikar's ship was becalmed, and they drew lots to determine who should be sacrificed to Wóden for favorable winds. Each time it came up King Vikar. It was at this point that Starkaðr was taken to a council of the gods. There, Wóden told him he wanted King Vikar. Can this be called a crime? True, Starkaðr killed his king, but it was Wóden's desire he do so, and Vikar was chosen by lot. In essence, Starkaðr changed his orlay by doing what Wóden wished him to do, and committing a crime that was not a crime. It would seem that while the Wyrdæ or the gods determine generalities, the specifics are left up to the individual. This, of course, is not conclusive, as it draws on one instance in one myth.

Similar to orlay is wyrd (pronounced roughly wurd). Scholars, on the topic of wyrd from an Old English perspective all see wyrd as being "blindly ruling Fate." B. J. Timmer's "Wyrd in Anglo-Saxon Prose and Poetry" is considered one of the most important studies on wyrd, and in his study, this is Timmer's conclusion. Wyrd, and thus one's orlay is unchanging, cannot be altered, and therefore denies free will. This does not always appear to be the case in the lore however. The word wyrd comes from proto-Germanic *werthan "to become." *Werthan in turn comes from proto-Indo-European *wert- "to turn, wind." Thus wyrd is that which is becoming. This would seem to indicate that wyrd unlike orlay is not set in stone. That is, it is ever changing, evolving from one moment to the next. We can make changes to our fate, or at least modify it. We are not stuck with what we are given at birth. Indeed, as we go through life we can make changes, and modify our orlay.

Given the example of Starkaðr's first heinous crime, the killing of King Vikar, we see that while we may be "fated" to do something, we still have the free will to control the circumstances. Perhaps it is easiest to look at wyrd or orlay in the terms of modern parlance. We all have coded into our DNA certain traits with which we are born. However, we can decide what to do with those traits. For example, I have brown hair because my DNA says I do. However, I can dye my hair red if I wish, and therefore change my appearance. Perhaps a better example is intelligence. Scientists have known for some time that some traits such as intelligence are inherited. However, what one chooses to do with their intelligence is entirely up to them. In essence, the Wyrdæ and perhaps the gods determine our orlay, but what we do with it is largely up to us.

It is difficult to often learn what you are fated to do. Some things are obvious such as one's intelligence, talents, physical prowess, but many things that Wyrd and her sisters laid down for us may not be. We may therefore have to be content not knowing. Regardless, we can always modify what we do. For example, I seem to have a talent for writing. What I do with that talent is largely up to me. I can be a lyricist for a rock band, write technical manuals, or books on Heathenry, or I can do all these things. Someone with a talent in music can decide what kind of music he or she wants to perform, what instruments they play, and whether they want to pursue a recording career. Despite some parts of your fate being predetermined, you still have a large amount of free will to do what you please.

The Sacred and The Holy

The ancient Heathens had not one, but two concepts of what were sacred and holy. One was that which is whole, healthy, and holy. Old English hálig (pronounced roughly holly), our modern word holy is related to our words health, hale, and whole. That which was holy to the ancient Anglo-

Saxon pagans was that which was healthy or whole. The other concept is that of the sacred. Old English wíh (pronounced weeh) "sacred site" is related to words that mean, "separate from the ordinary." Both hálig and wíh can be represented by the Latin words sanctus (Greek agios) and sacer (Greek hieros) respectively.

The idea of something being whole and healthy and therefore something sacred is a very old concept. Latin sanctus "holy" has its origins in the same proto-Indo-European words as Old English gesund (High German gesund). Old English gesund means "healthy, in good condition." The idea of health and wholeness being holy was widely used in the ancient Germanic tongues. Indeed, it seems to be the more important of the two concepts. The concept was used in a variety of ways. Old English hálsian (ON heilla) means, "to invoke spirits," while Old English háligern means, "sacred site." Old English hæleþ means "hero." All these words are related to our word holy.

Unlike hálig, wíh and its proto-Germanic ancestor *wíh- were pretty much used to mean, "separate, part of the realm of the gods." Proto-Germanic *wíh- comes from proto-Indo-European *vík- "to separate," and has a cognate in Latin vic- as in victima "sacrifice." As an adjectival prefix it survives today in German *Weihnacten* "the sacred nights" used of the Yule season. *Wíh- and words related to it all revolved around the idea of that which is separate from the ordinary or mundane. Such terms as Old English wíh (ON ve; OHG wíh) "sacred site;" wéoh "idol;" and Old Norse vigja "to consecrate" were some of the ways the concept was applied. That which was *wíh- is that which is somehow "otherworldly," or connects us to the worlds of the gods. The term was applied to words for cultic centers, temple sites, idols, and grave mounds.

There is a term that appears on Gothic ring of Pietroassa; wíhailag would seem to be a combination of the two concepts. Something that is wíhailag is something that is both "whole, healthy" and "otherworldly." This is expressed in other terms in the Germanic languages. Old Norse vé heilakt means the same thing, as does Old English sundorhálg.

Essentially, that which is hálig can be of the realms of Man or the gods, while that which is wíh is that of the realm of the gods. That which is holy is "whole, healthy," while that which is wíh is "otherworldly." Anything that is wíh has qualities of the gods' realms, and carries with it powers that leave Man in awe. Something that is wíh hálig is something that is particularly sacred.

When performing rites it is important to remember these two concepts. One's altar for example, a wéofod (pronounced way-oh-fod) is thought to be set apart from the ordinary. That is your altar because it connects you to the gods is, in a way, otherworldly. On the other hand when one hallows the food or drink they are using in a rite, they are trying to make it holy; whole, and free from fault. These two concepts of course can come together. One's wéofod can be both holy and wíh, wíhálig. You will see in the chapter on rites how these concepts come into play.

Inneryard and Outeryard

Another set of concepts that is important to Anglo-Saxon Heathenry is represented by the Old Norse terms innangarðs and úttangarðs. These terms can be represented by modern English inneryard and outeryard. The ancient Germanic pagans saw their farmsteads as separate from the wilds around them. Their farmsteads formed the inneryard. All outside of it was considered the outeryard. This idea does not only extend to physical locales however. It is also applied to society as well. An individual was a member of a family, and that family was thought of as an inneryard. The family was a part of a larger inneryard that of the clan, and the clan formed a part of an even larger inneryard, the tribe. This had important implications when it came to laws and customs.

The smallest unit in the Anglo-Saxon law codes was the family. If an individual committed a crime, it was the family that was held accountable because it formed an inneryard all its own. If the crime were severe enough, the whole clan might be held accountable. It was the tribe as the largest inneryard that made the laws through tribal custom and tradition. Each inneryard has their own laws and customs, and unless it is a part of a larger inneryard, no other inneryard's laws and customs can be applied to it. For example, the laws of the United States of America, an inneryard cannot be applied to that of the United Kingdom, another inneryard. The concept of inneryard plays a role in what is wíh. That which is wíh is that which is part of the inneryard of the gods, part of their realms, and therefore separate from the ordinary realms of Man.

Frith

In modern heathendom one often hears the word frith. As a concept dear to the hearts of our forebears, this is as it should be. Unfortunately, like so many words in our language, frith fell into disuse for several years, so that many modern heathen only barely understand its full meaning. To better understand the word frith, then, it may well be a good idea to look at both its origins and its meanings in Old English.

The word frith derives ultimately from Proto-Indo-European *priyas, "one's own (as in one's own kindred or one's community)." From this root also derived many other words, such as Old English fréodom (our modern word freedom), frigian ("to love"), and fréa ("lord," title of the god Ing), each with underlying connotations of belonging to a greater whole, such as a household or a community or a tribe--any group of people a person could call "one's own." According to John Clark Hall's "A Concise Anglo-Saxon Dictionary," the Old English word friþ meant: 1. peace, tranquility; 2. security, refuge; 3. privilege of special protection and the penalty for the breach of it; 4. the restoration of rights to an outlaw. The first meaning, "peace, tranquility," appears to be the way most heathens use frith today.

Deriving from PIE *priyas, frith's* original meaning was probably that of "the peace enjoyed while among one's own (that is, one's family or tribe)," this naturally led to secondary meanings of "security" and "refuge"--if a person cannot be safe among "one's own," then where can he or she be safe? Frith as the peace and security guaranteed by membership in a community can be seen in its meaning as "the restoration of rights to an outlaw." Among the ancient Germanic peoples an outlaw was someone who, having committed a crime, was declared as being outside the law, or no longer a part of society. As such he or she had no rights as an individual whatsoever, and outlaws could even be killed without fear of prosecution for murder. In restoring an outlaw his rights, he or she was then made a member of society once again; hence, he or she could once again partake of the frith.

In Old English and the other Germanic languages frith appears to have always carried with it connotations of "security, refuge," even when it was used to mean "peace." This is borne out by various compounds in which the word appears. The Old English word friþgeard basically meant "asylum, sanctuary" and appears to have been used for areas cordoned off for religious use. A friþgeard would then be any enclosed area specifically dedicated to the worship of the gods. From Icelandic sources we know that violence (beyond the violence necessary to perform sacrifices) was forbidden on holy ground, and there was no reason to believe that this was not true of the other Germanic peoples as well. With violence banned in holy places, then, a friþgeard would not only be a place of peace, but of security and refuge as well. Another compound, which utilizes both of the major meanings of frith, is the Old English word friþgield (in modern English, frithguild). In Anglo-Saxon England the frithguilds were groups of men charged with keeping the peace; as such they are the forerunner of both England's mediaeval watchmen and modern day police force. Essentially the frithguilds insured that the frith was not broken--that the community as a whole remained peaceful-- and in doing so insured that the community was a "secure refuge" for those who lived in it.

Frith's meanings of "peace" and "security," then cannot be separated. When used to mean "peace," frith still carries the sense of being secure and free from harm. Similarly, when used to mean "security," frith still carries with it the sense of being peaceful and free from violence or hostility. This concept has not entirely died out among the Germanic peoples, as today we are still inclined to refer to police officers as "peace officers."

Frith and Law

The implications of frith go farther than what it may seem by simply looking at the word's origins and meanings. To further understand frith we should perhaps examine its relationship to the concept of law. The elder heathen saw law as the collective customs of the tribe, developed out of the collective deeds of the tribe and set by the precedents of the past. This concept of law survives somewhat in English Common Law, as well as in the United States Supreme Court, who must base their decisions upon a precedent set in the past (the Constitution). As it is difficult to separate an individual's deeds from the individual, the ancient Germanic peoples also found it hard to separate the tribe's customs from the tribe; hence to some degree the law was seen as the tribe as well. Frith, as the state of peace and security, which allows the community to survive is then also a state that allows the law--the tribe and its customs--to survive. It is well, then, that police officers should be called "peace officers."

While the heathen concept of law still exists in the governments of all Germanic peoples, it does so beside a concept of law inherited from Christianity. This concept of law dictates that the "Law" is simply a set of regulations handed down by a higher power (that is, Yahweh). It is reflected in both the governments of the ancient Hebrews, where the monarchs (such as David and Solomon)--as Yahweh's representatives on Earth--could create laws simply by their decrees, and Renaissance Europe (particularly France), where monarchs ruled by "divine right." In heathen terms, law develops out of the past actions of the tribe, so that every past member of the tribe can be credited with its creation. In modern Judeo-Christian terms, on the other hand, law is simply a set of regulations handed down to society by a higher power (such as a governing body, like Congress, or an absolute monarch). It is perhaps well to call the former concept law and the latter concept statute.

The difference between law and statute can be seen better when viewed from the standpoint of preserving frith. As heathen law is both the collective deeds of the tribe and the tribe itself, it must by force be concerned with maintaining the peace and security of the tribe--literally the frith. While in theory statute should concern itself with the preservation of society, it is a fact that it does not always do so. As statute is simply the decrees of a single ruler or a group of rulers, there is little to stop those in power from instituting statutes that might well do violence to society. We need look no further than the absolute monarchs of Renaissance France, who lived in the luxury of a palace while the French peasants slowly starved to death in crude huts (it must be kept in mind that this eventually resulted in the French Revolution). While law must preserve the frith, statute does not necessarily need to do so.

Proof of this can be seen in the House Un-American Activities Committee (HUAC) hearings of the 1940s and 1950s. In theory, HUAC, as a committee of the United States Congress, operated under the principles of the Constitution (THE Law). In reality, they operated under a different set of rules (their own peculiar "statutes," many of which existed nowhere other than the Congressman's heads), often in direct conflict with the Constitution. Suspected Communists called before HUAC were more often than not presumed guilty until proven innocent, while innuendo and hearsay were sometimes sufficient "evidence" to "convict" an individual of Communism. Taking the Fifth Amendment could result in the individual being charged with "contempt of Congress," while a person's First Amendment rights to express his own political views often were ignored. Not only did all of this violate the Law (that is, it was unconstitutional), but it violated the peace and security--the frith--of many individuals as well. As a result of the HUAC hearings, many people lost their careers, some of whom in turn left the country or committed suicide. At the same time many Americans--guilty of no more than being a New Deal Democrat--were frightened to express their own political views for fear of being labeled a "premature anti-Fascist" or a "Left wing bleeding heart." Operating under their own "statutes," HUAC and other "Red baiting" individuals had compromised the frith of the United States.

    The conflict between law and statute can even be seen in today's attitudes towards officers of the law. The frithguilds of Anglo-Saxon England were essentially the forerunner of the modern day police department and can in many ways be considered an early equivalent. As the word friþgield shows, their primary duty was to see that the frith was not broken. They insured that members of the community continued to treat each other as "their own" and did not wreak havoc on each other as they might the member of an enemy community. The frithguild, then, saw that the community remained a peaceful, united whole, as opposed to disunited factions that were at constant war with each other. As keepers of the peace, the average Anglo-Saxon probably looked up to and respected the frithguildsmen as an important part of society.

    The modern day police department still retains some of the spirit of the frithguild. We still refer to police officers as "officers of the peace" and the phrase keeping the peace is still used of maintaining law and order. Unfortunately, as our society still retains the concept of statute or "law" as regulations handed down by a higher power, many Americans tend to view police officers not as keepers of the peace, but as enforcers of statutes handed down from on high. This view may well be compounded by the phrase law enforcement used to refer collectively to police officers, sheriffs, U. S. Marshals, G-Men--many people mistakenly equating law with statute. The end result of this view is both resentment and a lack of respect for officers of the peace, where the individual is apt to regard the police officer not as "one of the tribe" there to defend his right to peace and security, but as an "outlander" there to arrest him for violation of statute. Such feelings, no doubt, make the police officer's job harder to perform--a situation hardly conducive to preservation of the frith.

Grith

Grith is the peace kept between two different inneryards. It differs from frith in that there is no guarantee of security. It is not permanent and fixed like frith. Still, it is an important concept in modern Anglo-Saxon paganism. For modern Anglo-Saxon Heathenry to survive, groups must work together to move it forward. This may mean working together on research, referring folks in an area a group is not in to a group that is in that area, to more ambitious projects such as publishing books and periodicals.

Thews

Thew is an archaic modern English word meaning "virtue." The Anglo-Saxons held that certain traits were virtuous or thewful. Within Anglo-Saxon paganism there are three that are held to be the highest. These are called the Three Wynns or Joys, and were thought of by Garman Lord. They are:

Wisdom - Adherence to the ancient wisdoms of our religion.
Worthmind - The maintenance of a personal sense of honor.
Wealthdeal - Generosity with one's family and friends.

Beyond these are many other thews, most mentioned in the Norse list of maxims known as the "Havamal (which can be found in the "Elder Edda"). A few of the major ones are bravery, industriousness, hospitality, troth or loyalty, truth, friendship, moderation, neighborliness, and steadfastness. There are several other thews, but if you can keep these others will be covered as well.

Wisdom

Wisdom was highly prized by the ancient Anglo-Saxon pagans, and Germanic peoples in general. Knowledge of any kind was highly prized. Within the lore are lists of maxims, riddles, and tales of knowledge contests. Wisdom consists of many things: folk wisdom and common sense, reasoning, and the willingness to learn. Even the gods quest for wisdom. In the "Elder Edda," Wóden sacrificed himself by hanging on the world tree to win the wisdom of the runes. At another time, he gave one of his eyes for a drink from Mimer's Well, the well of memory. The "Havamal has this to say:

> Happy is he who hath in himself
> praise and wisdom in life;
> for oft doth a man ill counsel get

> when 'tis born in another's breast.
>
> (Olive Bray translation)

It also has this to say,

> A better burden can no man bear
> on the way than his mother wit;
> 'tis the refuge of the poor, and richer it seems
> than wealth in a world untried.
>
> (Olive Bray translation)

Modern Anglo-Saxon pagans too should seek wisdom. This can be done by reading scholarly works on the religion, discussing the ideas with others, and by seeking out knowledgeable teachers.

Worthmind or Honor

Honor for the ancient Anglo-Saxon pagans was not something that came from within. Indeed, for the ancient Heathen it was more akin to "fame" or "reputation." Honor was given to one by their community. Still one has to do good deeds in order for the community to deem that one has honor. This basically means keeping all the other thews or virtues. One has to be generous, loyal, brave, hospitable, and truthfully in order to have honor. If one is all of those things and more they will or should be deemed to have honor amongst other Heathens. Those that lie, steal, are abusive, greedy, and rude to guests will not be considered to have honor. Therefore, one must always think what others will think of their actions. Will the community see one's deeds in a favorable light?

Weathdeal or Generosity

Generosity was one of the highest virtues amongst

ancient Heathens. Ancient Heathenry was a gifting culture, gifts played an important role in their lives, and as such generosity is praised as almost the highest virtue. Kings were called beaggiefas "ring givers" in "Beowulf", as well as beaga bryttan, "breaker of rings." Arm rings were a primary means of wealth as they were made of gold and silver and other precious metals. In "Beowulf," Hróðgar gave Beowulf a banner, a helm, a coat of mail, and a sword (line 1020) in return for slaying Grendel. And the "Havamal" states:

> No man is so generous he will jib at accepting
> A gift in return for a gift,
> No man so rich that it really gives him
> Pain to be repaid.
> (W. H .Auden & P. B. Taylor Translation)

Gifts were not only given to friends and to others in return for deeds done on one's behalf, they were also given to those less fortunate. The "Havamal" has this to say:

> Two wooden stakes stood on the plain,
> On them I hung my clothes:
> Draped in linen, they looked well born,
> But, naked, I was a nobody
> (W. H .Auden & P. B. Taylor Translation)

And the Anglo-Saxon Rune Poem says:

> Giefu (Gift) is to men – glee and praise,
> Support and worship (worthiness) – and to every wretch
> Honor and sustenance – that they would otherwise be left without.

Exchanging gifts was thought to create a bond

between the two givers. If one were given a gift, they had to give something back in return, or do some deed in return. Not only this, but giving of a gift indicated that either a pledge was being made, or that friendship was desired. There was great power in the giving and getting of gifts. Gronbech had this to say,

> One might safely trust to the gift and give it full power to speak on one's behalf, for the soul in it would of itself reach in to the obligation, to honor, must bind luck and weave fate into fate, must produce will, or place a new element into it. Therefore, no power on earth can check the effect of a gift halfway, when it has once passed from hand to hand, and therefore, none can resist the spiritual effect of that which he has suffered to come too near.
> (Gronbech, "Culture of the Teutons", 59)

To be generous therefore was to create many bonds of friendship, as well as many obligations from others to one's self. This is why kings and lords gave gifts. It ensured that in time of need they could count on folk coming to their aid. Those that were miserly, of course, did not enjoy this advantage.

George F Jones in "Honor in German Literature," points out the tale of King Rorik, a miserly king told in Saxo's "Gesta Danorum":

> In one of them a hero named Hjalte tells of an avaricious king named Rorik, who has accumulated wealth instead of friends and then tries, unsuccessfully, to bribe his enemies to spare him. Because he has been unwilling to give arm rings to his friends, his enemies finally take all

> his treasure and his life too (Jones,
> "Honor in German Literature," page 4)

So what does generosity mean to the modern Heathen? Well, largely, the concept unlike other thews does not have to be handled differently due to changes in our host culture. Heathens can still exchange gifts much as in ancient times, and give to the less fortunate. The concepts and rules are the same. What is important is that we gift, and gift often.

Bravery

Boldness or bravery is seen extensively in the lore. It is at the heart of many tales such as those of Sigurd and Beowulf.

> Wyrd often spares the undoomed man if
> his courage holds. (Beowulf 572b-573)

We can bring boldness into our lives by facing life-threatening situations without letting fear take over. Once when I was driving at night, I went to pass a car. Just as I was even with it lights came on about fifty feet in front of me. Some fool had been running without their headlights on. I said a quick prayer to Wóden and managed to put my car between the car I was passing and the oncoming vehicle (who had enough sense to take the shoulder). The point is I did not panic. If I had, I may have swerved into the car I was passing or onto the shoulder the other car took and hit it head on. Instead I remained calm. Soldiers over in Afghanistan show bravery daily as they face the rigors of war. So do policemen, firefighters, and many others that must face danger.

Bravery does not mean being without fear however. Some of the most courageous wermen and women face danger with a great deal of fear, but do what needs to be done anyway. Boldness is acting on what one needs to do despite fear. The policeman facing an armed gunman, the solder in combat, and the firefighter entering a burning building probably all have fears for their safety. But they do what needs to be done anyhow.

For modern Anglo-Saxon pagans bravery means going through life not acting on our fears. Whether we are facing combat, climbing the face of a mountain, or simply just driving on the freeway we must not let fear govern our actions. We should almost never do anything out of fear (there are exceptions of course). Regardless, we should go through life being brave.

Industriousness

For the ancient Heathen the ability to work hard was a fact of life. Fields had to be tilled, planted, and harvested, and livestock tended. Those that were lazy or failed to get the work done that was needed were likely to starve to death. One had to get the fields in during the spring, and be ready to harvest them in the fall. Failure to do so could mean starvation, and if enough folk failed to do so, famine. There were many things that had to be done in ancient times to survive. And all of it was done by hand. In addition to tending the fields and livestock, cloth had to be made for clothing, wood had to be chopped for the winter, repairs made to the farmstead. Things we take for granted today were not easy then. For example, to make clothing the thread had to be spun, then it had to be woven into cloth, and finally it had to be cut and sewn into clothing. Tending the fields was similarly labor intensive. One had to till the fields in the spring, then the fields had to be planted, finally one had to harvest the fields. All of this was done by hand.

Today it is still important to work hard. Unless one is independently wealthy, one needs to make a living. It does not matter what you do, so long as you are able to support yourself and your family. If that means working as a stockman in a grocery store because that is the best job you can get, then there is no shame in it as long as you work hard. You should never be ashamed of doing a menial job because that is the best you can get. Any work is honorable work so long as you are supporting your family, or at least doing your best to. Being industriousness does not mean only working hard to make a living. Keeping your house clean, taking care of your children, taking care of the lawn are all things that need to be done. In addition, you should strive to help out your local Heathen community if there is one. This may mean organizing gatherings, helping prepare meals at gatherings, cleaning up after feast, doing the rites, or even taking care of the children so others can do their duties. If you do not have a local community you can still be diligent about doing your own rites. The gods and ancestors are not impressed by work that is left half done.

Hospitality

Hospitality or guestliness was perhaps the second highest thew in ancient Germanic culture right behind generosity. Indeed, for travelers it was needed for survival. There were no inns, hotels, or motels in ancient times. To have someplace to stay one had to rely often on the hospitality of strangers. The "Havamal" has several things to say on hospitality among them the following:

> He craves for water, who comes for refreshment,
> drying and friendly bidding,
> marks of good will, fair fame if 'tis won,
> and welcome once and again.

(Olive Bray translation)

Being hospitable involves many things. In ancient times, the guest was offered a drink when entering the home. If their clothes were wet due to inclement weather they were given dry clothes to wear. If it was cold outside the guest was offered a place by the fire. The guest was even fed and given a place to sleep if needed. Today it may mean welcoming others into your home for Heathen gatherings, preparing food for them, and giving them a place to sleep. Being a good host requires that one cater to every need of the guest. This includes entertaining them too. When you have a guest or guests you should not just sit them down in front of the TV (unless that is something they want to do). A host should entertain them with talk, even games. Hospitality is every bit as important today as it was in ancient times even though travelers' survival no longer depends on it.

Loyalty

Loyalty or troth was a highly prized virtue in ancient times. Members of war bands were ready to die with their leaders if that leader were killed in battle. Ancient Heathens stood by their family no matter what as well. The sentiment of troth can be seen in this passage from "Hrólf Kraki's saga:"

> In foul winds as in fair--- Keep faith with your lord, He who withheld no hoard for himself, but gave freely of gold and silver.

In ancient Anglo-Saxon England to betray one's family or friends was considered a great dishonor. Loyalty was highly prized. Today you should keep that in mind if you make an oath to a group or another individual. Consider whether or not these are people or a person you can be loyal to. Too many oaths of loyalty go broken today. Germanic Heathenry as a whole underrates this important thew.

Truth

Always speaking the truth and not lying is an important virtue. Lies, hearsay, and rumors can quickly destroy a group one is a part of. Words have power, and when one lies they are basing their deeds, and as a result their wyrd on falseness. This can only lead to disaster.

Therefore, you should always seek to be honest in what you speak and do. Even lies of omission can bring harm to others.

Friendship

Friendship means being able to treat one's friends as though they were family. It involves many of the other thews such as loyalty, truth, hospitality, and generosity among others. The "Havamal" has many things to say on friendship, among them are:

> If you find a friend you fully trust
> And wish for his good-will,
> exchange thoughts,
> exchange gifts,
> Go often to his house.
>
> (Olive Bray translation)

Friendship means desiring what is best for each other. It requires a certain degree of empathy, knowing what your friend wants. It also requires that you be sympathetic to your friend, that you understand his or her feelings and have compassion for him or her. This can require standing by him or her in bad times, and being the rock he or she can lean on or the shoulder he or she can cry on. It means having mutual understanding and compassion. Above all else it often means putting your friend's needs above your own.

One should always be honest with their friends. A friendship built on lies will not last long. This need not be brutal honesty. You should always keep your friend's feelings and interests at heart. But it does require that you be truthful. Even a truth that hurts will not hurt as much as a lie. This requires a degree of tact of course. Finally, friends should always exchange gifts. The ancient Heathens felt that gifts created bonds between two people or strengthened bonds that were already there.

A few good friends are better than many friends that you feel no kinship with. Life should not be a popularity contest. It is better to have a deep friendship, a good relationship with a few friends than mediocre relations with many people.

Moderation

Moderation means not doing anything in excess. This may mean eating less or drinking less. Too much of anything, even water can be a bad thing. The "Havamal" has several passages on being moderate in one's drinking, even being moderate in one's wisdom. The following is typical of its advice on drinking alcohol:

> Less good than they say for the sons of men
> is the drinking oft of ale:
> for the more they drink, the less can they think
> and keep a watch o'er their wits.

(Olive Bray translation)

And it has this to say on being moderate in speech:

> Let no man glory in the greatness of his mind,
> but rather keep watch o'er his wits.
> Cautious and silent let him enter a dwelling;
> to the heedful comes seldom harm,
> for none can find a more faithful friend
> than the wealth of mother wit.

(Olive Bray translation)

You should be moderate in everything. Many things we take as being good can be harmful if overdone. Too much exercise can lead to damaged joints and torn ligaments. Many vitamins that are healthy for us can become toxic if taken too often. Even water can be deadly if drank to excess (it can lead to a condition known as hyponatremia which is when the sodium in the body is diluted and cells fail to function properly). You should therefore not take things too far in anything you do.

Neighborliness

Being a part of a community requires you perform certain duties. This does not matter if it is your Heathen community or the neighborhood you live in. Being friendly towards those that you worship with and being friendly towards those you live around is important. The community we live in grants us a good part of our honor. This means you should always be kind to those that live around you. This may mean doing things like helping an elderly person take care of their home, or giving a ride to a neighbor when their car is the shop. Within your Heathen community, if you have one, it may mean the same things. You should always be kind to your neighbors.

Steadfastness

Steadfastness or tenacity is the refusal to give up. Life in ancient times was hard. With all the hard work, pain, and suffering it would have been easy for our ancient ancestors to give up on life, and quit trying. However, they did not, and that is why we are here now. Today, steadfastness is no less important. This may mean staying true to one's ways, or sticking with a job we hate just to support the family. Part of being steadfast is to keep trying. This may mean staying on a diet, keeping with quitting smoking, or completing a project. It can also mean staying true with friends and family when the going gets rough, standing by them in the worst of times. Being steadfast means not running away when things get hard.

Rites

Ritual Tools

In order to perform rites, you will need a set of tools. You will need a blessing bowl or blot bowl. This is a large bowl (a salad bowl works fine) that is specially dedicated to holding the liquid offering for the blessing (explained below). Once it is used for the blessing the liquid is then given to the gods and goddesses. You will also need a hlót-teinn, or a sprig used to sprinkle the liquid for the blessing. This can be a sprig of leaves taken from any tree. Most use sprigs from evergreens for this purpose. You will want to use a new one with each offering. If you plan to burn incense or raw herbs with your offering you will need an incense burner or a firepot. You will also need a drinking horn to drink from. If you do not have a drinking horn, a goblet will do. Some folks have an oath ring on their altar. An oath ring is a silver arm ring that oaths are sworn upon. Finally, you will need your altar or wéofod (pronounced way-oh-fod). These tools may be used for one purpose only, and that is to make offerings to the gods and goddesses. They should not be used for mundane purposes. You would not want to use your blot bowl to put salad in, or your altar as a coffee table. How these things are used will be explained below.

Altar Dedication

Your altar or wéofod will be the central focal point of your worship. On it will set your images of statues of the gods. An image or statue of a god or goddess is called a wéoh (pronounced way-oh). Also on it you may wish to place your ritual tools, and any amulets you may wear such as a Thor's hammer. Your wéofod should be in a prominent location where you can pass by it everyday. This serves as a reminder of the gods and goddesses. You do not want to hide it away in an unused or rarely entered room. Some rooms are not as good as others. One would not, for example, want to place their wéofod in a dirty workshop or a garage. Otherwise, any room you use regularly such as your living room or even kitchen would do. Your wéofod should be of sturdy construction, clean, and large enough to hold all your ritual tools and wéohas. A table would do or a chest. I have seen some use the mantle of a fireplace. I use a blanket chest for my wéofod, and store extra ritual tools inside it. By no means should it be used for anything else. A dresser top in which one has clothes would not make a good wéofod. A wéofod should be specially dedicated to the gods and goddesses or ancestors. It is where they come to visit you, their little space inside your home.

Some folks have more than one wéofod. And there is no reason that you cannot also. I have one dedicated to the gods and goddesses and another to the ancestors. On my gods altar I have my wéohas, my Thor's hammer necklace, a bag of runes, an oath ring, my blot bowl, and a lantern that I use to hallow offerings. On my ancestral altar I have pictures of my most immediate ancestors and keepsakes. One can also have smaller altars dedicated to the elves and cofgodas. These altars need not be as elaborate as those to the gods or ancestors and are unlikely to have any wéohas on them. If you wish you could have a wéofod specially dedicated to any deity you feel close to. I know of people that have a wéofod in every room.

Once you have acquired your ritual tools and statues or other representations of the gods, you will want to set up your wéofod. Start off by selecting your wéofod. It can be a table, chest, or any other raised flat surface you can set your tools and wéohas on. If you want, you can place an attractive cloth over it. If you are lucky enough to have room outside you can build one of stone. This kind of altar is called a hearg or harrow. You can also then set up god posts, a special kind of wéoh that is carved from a pole or trunk of a tree. One will still want an altar inside on which to keep their ritual tools least they get damaged by wind, rain, ice, or snow, but there are advantages to worshiping in the open air. Many feel closer to the gods and goddesses outside. You are not as limited on space, and often you can have a larger altar that way. Once you have your altar set up you will want to hallow it and dedicate it to the gods and goddesses.

The things you will need for this are a bottle of wine or mead or other liquid, a candle, your blot bowl, and a hlót-tán. First you will want to make the area sacred space. You can do this by circling the wéofod with a candle or torch and saying:

> Fire I bear around the frithyard
>
> And bid all men make peace
>
> Flame I bear to encircle this space
>
> And ask ill wights to fare away
>
> Þunor make sacred, Þunor make sacred
>
> Þunor make sacred this holy site.

Then call on Þunor as the hallower to make the altar sacred. Something simple like "Þunor please make this wéofod sacred" will suffice, although you could always do something more elaborate. Next you will want to hallow the liquid being used to bless the altar. Passing the horn or goblet over the candle's flame and saying, "Þunor please hallow this drink" can do this. Next you will want to do the wéofod's first offering calling on the gods to bless it and sprinkle it with mead or wine or other liquid you are using. Saying a short prayer asking the gods and goddess to bless the wéofod best does this. The prayer might go something like:

> Ése and Wen I call on you.
>
> Please bless this wéofod and make it holy.
>
> I dedicate its use to you.

And will do all I can to keep it holy.

With those words said, you can then sprinkle the altar with the liquid you have hallowed. Take the blot bowl outside and pour the liquid under a tree with the words. "Ése and Wen I give this to you." Your altar is now dedicated.

Composing a Prayer

One of the most understated ritual forms in modern Heathenry is the bede or prayer. Yet no other ritual can be performed almost anywhere. Whether it be atop some river bluff, in ritual space, or on a Greyhound bus headed east, a bede to the gods or ancestors can be said. Yet modern Heathens often do not seem to take the time, or exert the energy to compose ready made prayers that can be used in an offering or when the need arises. From experience I know this is only because most do not even know how to begin writing a bede. Prayer composition is not difficult. By examining the lore, looking at surviving bedes in the Eddas, and at the Anglo-Saxon charms, one can reliably reconstruct what the outline of a good Heathen prayer should look like.

The Outline

What few surviving prayers we have on hand reveal a definite structure. There is no way of knowing whether all ancient bedes followed this structure or only the ones that have survived. Never the less, a working outline for composing prayers can be formulated from several of the surviving bedes. A section of the Anglo-Saxon "Æcer-bót" (also known as the "Field Remedy" or "For Unfruitul Land") reveals a definite structure.

> Wes þú Hál, folde—fira módor;
> (wassail Earth—Mankind's mother)
> béo þú growende—in godes f?ðme,
> (be thou growing—in god's embrace)
> fódor gefylled—firum tó nytte.
> (With food filled—for men to use)

> beorht blówende—þú gebletsod weorþ.
> (bright blossoming—thou blessed worth)
> Þæs hálgan name—þe þás heofongescóp,
> (In that holy name—that the heaven shaped)
> ond þás eorðan—þe wé on lífiaþ,
> (and that of the earth—that we live in)
> sé god—sé þás grundas geworhte,
> (that god—that the grounds wrought)
> geunne ús—growende giefe
> (grant us—growing yield)
> þæt ús corna gehwilc—cume tó nytte.
> (that every kind of corn to us—comes to use)

This prayer opens with a greeting to the goddess Earth, and with the second line begins semi-mythical references to the marriage of Ing Fréa and Gerd, the union between Wóden and Eorðe that produced Þunor, or a similar union of some kind. It ends by petitioning for good harvests of every kind of crop.

Another surviving bede found in the "Sigdrífumál" from the "Elder Edda" reveals a similar structure:

> Hail Day, Hail, Sons of Day!
> Hail Night and New Moon!
> With kind eyes look hither and grant us
> Victory while we live.
>
> Hail Gods! Hail Goddesses!
> Hail bountiful Earth!
> Grace us both with the gift of speech
> And leech hands while we live.
> (W H Auden & P B Taylor Translation.)

The prayer begins by hailing Dæg, his children, Niht and Mona. It then asks that they grant victory. Finally the prayer hails the gods and goddesses and asks for the gift of speech and healing hands.

Both prayers follow the same general pattern. The Æcer-bót passage as part of a larger rite includes mythological references, along with further petitioning. The Sigdrífumál bede on the other hand lacks mythological references, but still hails the gods and makes a request. Both have the same basic structure, although one is a quick prayer that is meant to stand alone, the other a more elaborate part of a larger rite.

Another simple prayer that seems to follow the same pattern is one recorded by Ibn Fadlan done by one of the Rus.

> "Oh my lord, I have come far with many slave-girls and many sables ....Now With these offerings I come to you....Send me a merchant with lots of gold and willing to buy on my terms." (Dunn translation)

This prayer follows close to the pattern. The Rus merchant greets his god, he then proceeds to list what he is about to give his god, and finally petitions for a merchant willing to buy at his price. This prayer differs in that the merchant does not mention any mythological references, but instead lists what he is offering the god in return for his request. Finally, a portion of a prayer to Thor survived in Snorri's "Skáldskaparmál" in the "Elder Edda." All that remains are the mythological references. However, these are enough to let us know such references were made.

> You smashed the limbs of Leikn,
> you bashed Þrivaldi;
> you knocked down Starkaðr;
> you trod Gjalp dead under foot.

Drawing on the bedes and fragments of bedes above, one can reconstruct an outline for prayers as such: 1) A greeting to the god or gods. 2) A boast of the god or gods' great deeds, or other mythological references. In addition, the deities were invoked through various hight names (other names for the gods and goddesses they go by) and by names as in the "Æcer-bót." 3) A petition or request. This was most likely simple, in "Víga-Glúms saga" Þórkell with the gift of an ox, simply asked that the man who expelled him from his lands be done likewise. The prayer was simple and effective as the ox fell over dead, and the man was expelled.

Variations of this outline can be used. The Sigdrífumál in fact merges two prayers into one, while the Rus prayer recounted by Ibn Fadlan contains no mythological references, but instead states what the Rus merchant is offering in sacrifice. Armed with this outline, one can then begin to tackle the fairly easy task of prayer composition.

Composition in English and Old English

Nothing says you need to perform your prayers in Old English, In fact, most Anglo-Saxon pagans probably do not. But many enjoy the sound of the old tongue, and therefore write and perform bedes in Old English. In the back you will fine a list of resources for learning Old English. Before writing in Old English, you will want to obtain a good grammar and dictionary. Any number of grammars will do, but make sure you get one that teaches early Old West Saxon and not Late West Saxon. There are subtle vowel differences, which will make composing difficult with Late West Saxon. As for dictionaries I recommend you get Clark Halls' which is the best affordable dictionary out. Finally, Stephen Pollington's *Wordcraft*, which is available, is an invaluable English to Old English dictionary and thesaurus. For composition in English, a good thesaurus often comes in handy for keeping to alliterative verse. Wordlists terms specific to our religion are also handy as are a list of kennings (a kenning is a couple of words that employ figurative speech to name what they are describing) and hight names of the gods. A hight name is another name or title that a god or goddess goes by. An example of this is Wóden is sometimes called Eallfæder "All Father," while Þunor is sometimes called Buccadod "he-goat god." A couple of examples of hight names from the "Æcer-bót" for the goddess Eorðe are Folde "Earth" and fira módor "Mankind's mother."

As to verse and meter, modern Heathenry like its ancient counterpart has enjoyed the use of alliterative verse or stave rhyme. In alliterative poetry the stress or emphasis falls on words that begin with the same consonant or sometimes vowel. The number of stressed and unstressed syllables of a line of poetry is kept track of by the poetic meter or rhythm. Meter measures the number of stressed and unstressed syllables, as well as when and where they appear. Old Lore Meter was the most common ancient meter. It is best known from "Beowulf," and consists of two half-lines linked by words that alliterate in each half-line. Each half-line consists of at least two stressed syllables and a variable number of unstressed syllables. The last stressed syllable of the last half-line may not alliterate, in Old Lore Meter or any other.

Composing in something like Old Lore Meter is difficult using modern English, but can be done. An example of something close to Old Lore Meter is a translation of the first line of the rune-verse Dæg (Dagaz) of the "Anglo-Saxon Rune Poem." Alliterating consonants are in bold.

Day is the **drighten's** herald **dear** to man.

As can be seen by the above line, something close to Old Lore metre is not difficult to use. Other meters, such as the Eddic ljóðaháttr ("song-meter"), are much harder to work with. Lóðaháttr alternates between two half-lines and one full line, with stanzas of four half-lines and two full lines. The half-lines are like those of Old Lore meter, while the full lines must have three stresses, of which two alliterate. The "Havamal," for the most part, is written in lóðaháttr. Similar to lóðaháttr is galdralag (enchantment-order); it follows the pattern of lóðaháttr, except that it repeats one of the full lines (sometimes with minor variations) meters at the end of a stanza. There are also several skaldic meters but these for the most part are nearly impossible to use in modern English and not easily used in Old English.

If one is wishing to learn to compose in Old English, some practical advice to follow is make your first attempts in English and then translate them to Old English. This helps one build a vocabulary, and to learn the grammar involved. Avoid pronouns, as they were not often used in Old English poetry and try to stick to words of Anglo-Saxon descent. A dictionary will give the origins of most words. A good resource to use is the Online Etymology Dictionary at http://www.etymonline.com/. You simply type in a word and it then gives you a short definition and then gives the origin of the words. By using words of Anglo-Saxon origin you make translating easier. It is best to worry less about the meter in the beginning, and more about simply getting the alliteration down pat. The meter only comes with time and practice; first one must build a vocabulary, and learn grammatical structure. I rarely get the meter right, and I have been composing prayers in English and Old English for twenty years. Finally, read alliterative poetry in modern English, and if possible many of the ancient poems. This sets in one's mind the patterns used in composition.

Composing a Prayer

Once one has settled on an outline and studied the formats of the ancient poetry, one can easily set down and compose a prayer. A prayer is a highly personal thing, and while you may have made many objective observations in learning how to compose a bede in authentic Heathen fashion, you will want to apply this method to the actual words you want to say. That is the words must come from your heart. Repeating by rote parts of the Eddas or other ancient works, while not a bad thing, is not nearly as moving as words that spring from your own soul, your own relationship with the Gods.

For those that do not write or are not poets, this can be difficult. We are not accustomed today to getting in touch with deep spiritual feelings. You may find that when you try to compose a prayer the words just will not come, or sound trite. Do not worry; the words for your bede will come to you... sometimes at an odd or inconvenient time. I have had inspiration hit me on buses, driving the car, on walks in the woods, and even at work. Once you are inspired and begin composing a prayer use the same tools our spiritual forbears did. Kennings and hight names come in handy when you are unable to think of an alliterating line of your own, tales from the Eddas and the Icelandic sagas told in your own words can be used to fill in gaps, and finally the use of your own experiences with the gods make prime prayer material. If you find that the words for a prayer do not come to you, try meditating on what it is you want to say. Soon you will be able to say what you wish to the gods or ancestors in a poetic fashion. Everyone can compose their own bedes given time. Only in this way, will perhaps the most effective, yet easiest rite in Anglo-Saxon paganism find its rightful place.

Making Offerings

The rite you will perform most often is called an offering or a gield (modern English yield). This rite is fairly simplistic in its workings, but at the same time its metaphysical parts are rather complex. There are four kinds of offerings; there are libations (the offering of liquids), food offerings, object offerings, and blót (pronounced bloat). Libations are when a liquid such as milk, wine, or mead are offered. Food offerings are when something eatable is offered. Object offerings are when something such as a sword or jewellery are offered. And finally, blót is when a live animal is offered up to the gods and goddesses. The mechanics for each is roughly the same.

The Purpose of Offering

The purpose of offerings is to thank the gods for gifts received or to ask for more gifts. This is touched upon in the Norse lore. In "Fjölsviðmál," it is said:

> Tell me, Fjolsvith, for I wish to know;
> answer as I do ask do they help award to
> their worshippers, if need of help they
> have?
>
> Ay they help award to their worshippers,
> in hallowed stead if they stand; there is
> never a need, that neareth a man but
> they lend a helping hand. (Hollander
> translation)

And in "Hynduljóð" it is said:

> He a high altar made me Of heaped
> stones-all glary have grown The
> gathered rocks-and reddened anew
> them with neats' fresh blood; for ay
> believed Óttar in the ásynjur. (Hollander
> translation)

Similar accounts appear in the Icelandic sagas. In *Víga-Glúms Saga*, Þorkell states Frey had "accepted many gifts from him" and "repaid them well." While we do not have much information on how the Anglo-Saxons viewed offerings there is little doubt that it was much different from how the Norse viewed them. Old English gieldan meant, "to pay for, reward, requite," and also "to worship, to sacrifice to." Thus, one of the main reasons to make offerings was to exchange gifts with the gods.

When gifts were exchanged, the ancient Heathens thought it formed a bond. Vilhelm Grönbech had this to say on gift exchanges:

> When an article of value is passed across the boundary of frith and grasped by alien hands, a fusion of life takes place, which binds men one to another with an obligation of the same character as that of frith itself." (Grönbech. *The Culture of the Teutons*, Vol.2, p. 55)

This is confirmed by verses in the "Havamal:"

> Not great things alone must one give to another, praise oft is earned for nought; with half a loaf and a tilted bowl I have found me many a friend.
>
> (Bray translation)

> Hast thou a friend whom thou trustest well, from whom thou cravest good? Share thy mind with him, gifts exchange with him, fare to find him oft.
>
> (Bray translation)

There is little reason to think that the ancient Heathens saw this as being any different with the gods. Just as men were bonded to each other through the exchange of gifts so too were men and gods bonded by the exchange with gifts. When you make an offering to the gods you connect with them in a special way. By giving to the gods, you make them a part of your world, a part of the human community.

Making an offering is also a form of communion. That is your thoughts and feelings are shared with the gods when making an offering, and the gods' thoughts and feelings are sometimes shared in return. A sense of oneness is felt with the gods when doing an offering. Discussing passages on blót Turville-Petre notes:

> "The meaning of the sacrificial feast, as Snorri saw it, is fairly plain. When blood was sprinkled over altars and men and the toasts were drunk, men were symbolically joined with gods of war and fertility, and with their dead ancestors, sharing their mystical powers. This is a form of communion." (Turville-Petre. *Myth and Religion of the North*, p. 251).

In addition to serving as a form of communion, offerings also serve as a way of conveying one's wants and desires to the gods. In ancient times in times of famine or pestilence no doubt appeals were made to the gods for help. Often times you will convey personal desires to the gods. An example of this is seen in the Norse lore. In "Víga-Glúms Saga," Thorkell offers Frey an ox with a request for revenge on the man that had taken his land. In an account by the Arab trader Ibn Fadlan Rus traders are said to have made offerings to the gods to gain more customers. The "Æcer-bót," an Anglo-Saxon rite found in the manuscript called the "Lacnunga" contains Christianised Heathen prayers asking for fertility of the land. Offerings are a way of communicating one's wishes, needs, and desires to the Ése, Wen, elves, and ancestors.

  An offering then may serve many purposes. It may be a way to give thanks to the gods or ancestors. It may also be a way to communicate one's wishes to the gods or ancestors along with a petition asking for help. Finally, offerings are a way to create bonds with the gods, a way to connect with them and create a relationship with them. It is a way of letting your feelings and thoughts known to them, and trying to figure out their feelings and thoughts.

Offerings in Ancient Times

There are two primary accounts of how offerings were made in ancient times. One is from the Norse lore, and the other from the Anglo-Saxon lore. The Norse account comes from "from Hákonar Saga goða," a part of the "Heimskringla:"

> It was an old custom, that when there was to be sacrifice all the bondes should come to the spot where the temple stood and bring with them all that they required while the festival of the sacrifice lasted. To this festival all the men brought ale with them; and all kinds of cattle, as well as horses, were slaughtered, and all the blood that came from them was called "hlaut", and the vessels in which it was collected were called hlaut-vessels. Hlaut-staves were made, like sprinkling brushes, with which the whole of the altars and the temple walls, both outside and inside, were sprinkled over, and also the people were sprinkled with the blood; but the flesh was boiled into savoury meat for those present. The fire was in the middle of the floor of the temple, and over it hung the kettles, and the full goblets were handed across the fire; and he who made the feast, and was a chief, blessed the full goblets, and all the meat of the sacrifice. And first Odin's goblet was emptied for victory and power to his king; thereafter, Niord's and Frey's goblets for peace and a good season. Then it was the custom of many to empty the brage-goblet; and then the guests emptied a goblet to the memory

of departed friends, called the remembrance goblet.

From this account we can deduce the following things: 1) the drinking horns or goblets were blessed 2) the people were blessed 3) prayers or fulls were made to the gods. The Æcer-bót contains a slightly different method of giving to the gods, one that is better with objects or small food items such as cakes. It is as follows (note it has been heavily Christianized):

> Here is the solution, how you may improve your fields if they are not fertile, or if anything unwholesome has been done to them through sorcery or witchcraft.
>
> At night, before dawn, take four turfs from the four quarters of your lands, and note how they previously stood. Then take oil and honey and yeast and milk from every cow that is in the land, and part of every kind of tree grown on the land, except hard beams, and part of every identifiable herb except the buckbean only, and add to them holy water.
>
> Then drip it three times on the base of the turfs, and say these words: Crescite, grow, et multiplicamini, and multiply, et replete, and fill, terre, this earth. In nomine patris et filii et spiritus sancti sit benedicti. And say the Lord's Prayer as often as the other.
>
> And then take the turfs to church and let a priest sing four masses over them, and let the green surface be turned towards the altar, and then, before sunset, let the

turfs be brought to the places where they were previously. And let the man have four crosses of quickbeam made for him, and write upon each end: Matthew and Mark, Luke and John. Lay the crucifix on the bottom of the pit, then say: Crux Matheus, crux Marcus, crux Lucas, crux sanctus Iohannes. Then take the turfs and set them down there, and say these words nine times, 'Crescite' as before, and the Lord's Prayer as often, and then turn eastward, and humbly bow down nine times, and then say these words:

Eastward I stand, entreating favours,
I pray the glorious Lord, I pray the great Lord,
I pray the holy warden of heaven,
Earth I pray and heaven above
And the steadfast, saintly Mary
And heaven's might and highest hall
That by grace of God I might this glamour
Disclose with teeth. Through trueness of thought
Awaken these plants for our worldly profit,
Fill these fields through firm belief,
Make these fields pleasing, as the prophet said
That honour on earth has he who dutifully
deals out alms, doing God's will.

Then turn yourself three times awiddershins, then stretch out flat and there intone the litanies. Then say; Sanctus, sanctus, sanctus to the end: then sing the Benedicte with arms extended, and the Magnificat, and the

Lord's Prayer three times, and commend it to Christ and Saint Mary and the Holy Cross, for love and for reverence, and for the grace of him who owns the land, and all those who are under him. When all that is done, then take unfamiliar seeds from beggars and give them twice as much as you took from them, and let him gather all his plough apparatus together; then let him bore a hole in the plough beam and put in there styrax and fennel and hallowed soap and hallowed salt. Then take the seed, set it on the plough's body, then say:

Erce, Erce, Erce, Mother of Earth,
May the Almighty grant you, the Eternal Lord,
Fields sprouting and springing up,
Fertile and fruitful,
Bright shafts of shining millet,
And broad crops of barley
And white wheaten crops
And all the crops of earth.
May God Almighty grant the owner,
(And his hallows who are in heaven),
That his land be fortified against all foes,
And embattled against all evil,
From sorceries sown throughout the land.
Now I pray the Wielder who made this world
That no cunning woman, nor crafty man,
May weaken the words that are uttered here.

Then drive forward the plough and cut the first furrow, then say:

Hail, Earth, mother of all;

Be abundant in God's embrace,
Filled with food for our folk's need.

Then take all kinds of flour and bake a loaf as broad as a man's palm, and knead it with milk and holy water, and lay it under the first furrow. Then say:

Field filled with food, to feed mankind,
Blooming brightly, be you blessed,
In the holy name of He who made
heaven, and earth on which we live, May
the God who made these grounds grant
to us his growing gifts That each kind of
seed may come to good.

Then say three times, Crescite in nomine patris, sit benedicti. Amen and the Lord's Prayer three times

From this one can come up with the following outline: 1) blessing of the gifts to be given 2) ritual actions and prayers 3) the first prayers 4) the driving of the plow through the field 5) the second prayer 6) the offering.

Offerings in Modern Times

Using the Norse account above, and other accounts found in the Norse lore, we can reconstruct what an offering should look like. To perform this offering, you will need your blot bowl, a hlót-tán, your horn, and a candle or other open flame.

1) The Creation of Sacred Space: You will first want to set aside ritual space. We know from the Icelandic "Landnámabók" that temple sites were circled with fire prior to the temples being constructed and used. Therefore, with a candle or torch you should circle the area you are going to use saying the following:

> Fire I bear around the frithyard
> And bid all men make peace
> Flame I bear to encircle this space
> And ask ill wights to fare away
> Þunor make sacred, Þunor make sacred
> Þunor make sacred this holy site.

2) Hallowing: You then hallow the food and/or drink by passing them over the flame of the candle or torch as we are told in account above. This can be done with the words "Þunor make sacred this food and drink." Prior to doing this you will want to pour the mead, wine, or other liquid into the blot bowl, and the horn or goblet.

3) Blessing: You then perform the blessing sprinkling the wine or mead or other drink on yourself and any others present with the hlót-tan.

4) The Prayers: You then say the prayers to the gods, goddess, or god one is making the offering to. Prayers in ancient times appear to have followed a general structure of a. greeting the deity b. a short telling of a myth about the god or goddess c. giving thanks or asking for help. Prayers are provided for each of the holytides later in this book.

5) The Myne or Toasts to the Ancestors: You then make a toast to your ancestors. If you are doing this as part of a group, then each person present can drink to their ancestors. If alone, you can drink to a particular ancestor or all your ancestors.

6) The Húsel or Housel: At this point you consume part of the food or drink. Take a drink of the mead, wine, or other liquid you are giving from the drinking horn, and eat a part of any of the food you are giving. You need not drink or eat much. In fact, it is better not to as this leaves more for the

gods. When you are through drinking from the horn, pour the remaining liquid into the blot bowl.

7) The Yielding: Finally, one gives the offering. Ideally, an offering is done outside, and if so the offering can be poured out at the base of a tree. If done inside, it can be saved for a later time, and then given to the gods outside. If you are living in an apartment and have no way to give an offering outside, it may be best to wait and make a libation in a public park (since leaving food may well be against the law).

A slightly different outline can be made from the Anglo-Saxon account.

1) Preparation: In this portion of the rite outline, you prepare whatever you may need for the rite. Bake bread, prepare turfs such as in the Æcer-bót, or obtain mead.

2) Blessing of gifts to be given: Here we are going to see part of the Norse outline. Although holy water (water drawn from a spring or brook before sunrise on a Spring morning) may be used instead of wine or mead. Most modern Heathens would probably prefer the use of mead. Just as in the Norse account the items would be blessed by sprinkling them with water or mead with the hlót-tán.

3) Creation of sacred space: One will do this in the same way as in the outline above.

4) Ritual Actions: You then turn counter clockwise three times and lay prostate on the ground, and say prayers to three deities. The content of these prayers is unknown, and the Christian substitutions give us no clues. The only possible clue they may give is these are prayers commonly used by Christians for protection. But more than likely they were an invite to the gods and goddesses.

5) The First Bede or Prayer: This prayer is the first of the major two prayers of the rite. This bede if one follows the

Æcer Bót is a song of praise. The god or goddess is greeted with the traditional greeting of "wassail" which generally is followed by praise of the deity.

6) More Ritual Actions: As we are trying to create a general ritual action, you need not drive a plow through your yard. But you will need to dig a hole. This hole is where one will put the offering being given to the gods.

7) The Second Bede or Prayer: A shorter bede in praise of the god or goddess you giving are the gifts to takes place here.

8) Yielding: You pour the mead or place the bread or other object in the hole and follow this with a prayer asking for gifts from the god or goddess. You then cover the hole with dirt.

Which outline you use is largely up to you. I have always felt the one based on the "Hákonar Saga goða" is best for food and drink offerings while the one based on the "Æcer-bót" works best for the offering of objects (especially if they are buried). Regardless, you can use either outline as they are both extremely flexible and can easily adapted to nearly any kind of offering.

Symbel

The other major rite besides offering of Anglo-Saxon paganism is symbel (pronounced roughly s-eww-m-bel). Symbel is a series of drinking rounds consisting of toasts, oaths, boasts, songs, stories, and even jokes. It is not so much a rite to the gods and goddesses as it is a rite of community building. Symbel is referenced several places in the lore. The main source is the epic poem "Beowulf," but it is also mentioned in the Old Saxon poem "Heliand," the Anglo-Saxon poem "The Dream of the Rood," the Anglo-Saxon poem "Judith," the Old Icelandic poem "Lokasenna," the Old Icelandic poem "," as well as some of the Icelandic sagas.

Paul Bauschatz, in his scholarly work "The Well and the Tree" theorizes that the purpose of symbel was to place one's self into the flow of Wyrd. Through symbel we can get in touch with Wyrd, and thus be able to help form it. Past deeds are boasted of, and oaths are made to do even greater deeds. When one boasts of past deeds they are doing what is known as a gielp (pronounced roughly yi-eh-lp). A gielp is a recitation of one's ancestry, and then a boast of a past deed. For example, I might say, "I am Swain, son of Albert and Rosie. I have written many books and articles. An oath to do an even greater deed is called a béot (pronounced roughly bay-oh-t). A béot is when someone oaths to do something difficult that they perhaps have never done before. For example I might make a béot something like this, "I will write a new beginners' book on Anglo-Saxon paganism." A béot is never made without a gielp, while a gielp can be made alone. You rarely hear a béot in symbel because they are quite serious and there are dire consequences for failing to complete one. You will often hear a gielp however. Folks enjoy boasting of their past accomplishments. By boasting of their past accomplishments they are ensuring through their wyrd that they will achieve similar accomplishments in the present and future.

Symbel revolves around deeds, past and present, and those yet to come. This is because it is deeds that formulate our wyrd. In the first symbel of "Beowulf," Beowulf states who his father was, and then proceeds to tell of the many great deeds he has done. He then makes an oath to slay the monster terrorizing Héorot. Having made his gielp and béot, Beowulf is not done. Unferþ the þyle (more on what a þyle is later) then challenges Beowulf's oath. Beowulf then restates his oath, and adds a tale of a swimming contest in which his life was in mortal peril, which he won. All of this was done to set Beowulf up for his deed yet to come, slaying the monster Grendel. Beowulf ends all of this with "Gað a wyrd swá hío sceol" (always go Wyrd as she shall). One's wyrd is based on the results of past deeds, and by stating these deeds in symbol, one is trying to ensure that future deeds have similar good results.

There is other significant speech of symbol. It is not all boasts and oaths. The gods and ancestors are toasted, and poets or scop tell tales of past events. The scholar Dwight Conquergood feels that the poets made the collective gielp or boast of the tribe. The seriousness of boasts and oaths are shown that they were done before battle such as in the Anglo-Saxon poem "The Battle of Maldon."

There are certain positions or "offices" of symbel. There is the host called a symbelgifa (pronounced roughly s-eww-m-bel- giva) "symbel giver." A symbelgifa acts as sort of a "master of ceremonies" approving or disapproving of boasts and oaths, and generally being the genial host. He or she is aided by the ealubora (e as in at- a as in baa u as in pull-l-b-o as in body-r-a) or "ale bearer." The ale bearer is in charge of making sure the mead or other drink is dispensed to those at the symbel. Generally, they are the wife or sister of the host. The ealubora is always female and always pours the first drink of symbel. Because women are in better touch with the Wyrdæ (who are female), it is thought that by pouring the first drink, those drinking from the horn or goblet will be closer in touch with their wyrd and orlæg. The ale bearer encourages people making boasts and oaths with compliments and flattery. She also keeps the peace by defusing tense situations.

Bryles (pronounced roughly brooles) or "horn bearers" assist the ealubora. Once the first drink is poured by the ealubora, a byrle takes over. A byrle is usually a young adult male or female that goes around to people and makes sure their horns are always full. The other important office besides symbelgifa and ealubora is the þyle (pronounced roughly thoole). The þyle challenges anyone who they feel makes an oath that cannot or the þyle feels cannot be completed. The þyle does this by pointing out the shortcomings of the person making the oath, and the þyle then states why they feel the oath will not be completed. The person making the oath can, of course, point out the short comings of the oath, explain why what the þyle feels are shortcomings are not, and then restate their oath. Other offices you might see at symbel are the scop and gléoman (pronounced roughly glay-o-man). The scop recites tales, sometimes myths of the gods, or tales of the group gathered at symbel if they are an organized group. The gléoman sings songs to entertain those gathered at symbel.

The Order of Symbel

While symbel appears in many sources, in each case we only see a part of the rite. We therefore need to piece together the rite from a variety of sources. In the Old Icelandic "Fagrskinna," we are told that toasts were made to the gods. In "Heimskringla," Sveinn drank to his father at his father's funeral symbel. Gift giving played a role. In the second symbel in "Beowulf," Hróðgar gave Beowulf a banner, a helm, a coat of mail, and a sword. Finally, significant speech is made at the opening of symbel, and during it.

The following outline is taken in part from Eric Wódening's article "An Anglo-Saxon Symbel," Steve Pollington's academic work "The Mead-Hall," and Paul Bauchatz's academic work "The Well and the Tree." Symbel is always done inside. The reason for this is that it must take place in the contained space of an inneryard. Wyrd according to the scholar Paul Bauscatz operates in a contained space. The home or hall in which the symbel is given represents this. Symbel almost always involves the drinking of alcohol. There is nothing to stop someone from using a non-alcoholic drink however. Often in my group if someone has to drive, or otherwise cannot drink alcohol they will drink juice or tea.

1) Symbelgifa Forespeech: Once everyone is seated the symbelgifa opens symbel. In "Beowulf," Hróðgar states "Sitaþ nu to symle ond onsælaþ meoto, sigehreð secgum, swa þin sefas hwettaþ (Sit now to symbel and unwind your

measures, victory hearted heroes)."

2) Ealubora Forespeech: The ealubora then enters with the horn or goblet of mead or other drink and brings it to the symbelgifa. In "Beowulf," Welatheow, Hróðgar's queen says:

> "Onfoh þissum fulle, freodrihten min,
> sinces brytta! þu on sælum wes,
> goldwine gumena, ond to Geatum spræc
> mildum wordum...
>
> Take this full, my lord war band leader,
> hoard sharer, you be happy, warriors'
> gold friend, and speak to the Geats with
> mild words..."

She then pours drink for each participant and then takes her seat by the symbelgifa. While pouring the drinks she should say something favorable to each person. After this the byrle takes over pouring the drinks for the rest of symbel.

3) Bregofull: The symbelgifa then hails the three most poplar gods or goddesses, and if a part of an organized group makes a boast of the group's future plans. Alternatively, each participant can toast the god or goddess of his or her choice.

4) The Myne: Each participant then toasts one of their ancestors or their ancestors in general.

5) Gift giving (optional): Gifts can then be exchanged beginning with the symbelgifa and the ealubora.

6) The Fulls: After the opening rounds, each participant can make a toast, make a boast, do a gielp and béot, sing a song, recite a poem, or do anything else that seems appropriate. The fulls can go on until the symbelgifa decides to end the

symbel. Most symbels I have been to have lasted six or seven rounds (including the forespeechs, bregofull, myne, and fulls). However, I have been to a few that lasted up to twenty rounds.

There is a less formal form of ritual drinking rounds called gebeorscipe. This can be done outside, and lacks the many formal opening rounds. There are not hard and fast rules for gebeorscipe other than the first round is generally to the gods, and the second round to the ancestors.

Some Rules for Symbel

As symbel involves the drinking of alcohol it pays well to have some rules in place.

1) The peace of a symbel is sacred. No one should commit a violent act during symbel, and if they do, they should be expelled immediately.

2) Participants should not get drunk. Symbel is not a drinking game. Its aim is not to get drunk despite its use of alcohol. And absolutely no one should drive drunk. Those participating in symbel should be prepared to stay where the symbel is being held unless they have a sober person to drive them, or can walk to where they need to go or take public transportation.

3) If, in a state of drunken zealousness you make a boast the symbelgifa or þyle feels you cannot keep, try to prove them wrong and do what you oathed to do. DO NOT hold a grudge against someone for doing their religious duty in symbel, even if they allowed personal prejudice to affect their judgment. In such a case, by your behaving honorably, it is their honour that is lessened not your own, and they are not likely to challenge you again in symbel. Too, remember that a symbel's frith is rigidly enforced. Open debate is welcome, and even pointing out flaws in someone's honor with insults, but half-truths, flat out mockery of honorable actions, and

lies are not. And few true Heathen would have a problem with someone expounding such being asked to go outside, as Þunor did Loki in the "Lokasenna."

4) Do not make passes at married ale bearers or the spouse of another. Causal flirting is okay, but it might be good to keep this line of the "Havamal" in mind: "Be especially wary of ale and of another man's wife." This goes for ladies too. Alcohol and anything beyond flattery can bring on jealousy and a fight.

A Few More Words on Symbel

Symbel is one of our most sacred rites. It should be approached with the utmost seriousness. When preparing for symbel one should consider what they want to drink. Mead, ale, beer, wine, hard cider are all acceptable. One should always have non-alcoholic drinks for those that do not drink alcohol or cannot drink alcohol. Sweet cider, juice, and even tea are all acceptable. I find drinks high in vitamin C work best as vitamin C can offer an altered state of its own, though different from alcohol. Of course, tea and coffee contain caffeine, which also offers an altered state. Many groups like to use home brewed mead, and will exhaust that supply before moving onto something store bought.

Conclusion

One should try to do an offering on each holy tide, and symbel as often as possible. If you are solitary then symbel cannot be done. Symbel cannot be done alone, although one can certainly drink toasts to the gods, ancestors, and such on their own, and then offer up the remainder of the drink to the gods and ancestors. The rites presented here are designed to be done alone or with a group. In the next chapter on holy tides a sample rite will be given for each one (in some cases more than one rite will be offered). Feel free to use these, modifying them if you have to.

Holy Tides

There are several holy tides in Anglo-Saxon paganism and different people celebrate different ones. So here I am giving the most common ones. This list is not all-inclusive, and you will encounter other holy tides. And you can certainly offer rites at other special times such as mundane holidays (for example Independence Day in the USA). With each holy tide I have a sample rite. Feel free to use the sample rites as you see fit, at least until you feel competent to write your own. Some folks like to compose their prayers for rites before hand; others like to say their prayers off the cuff during the rites. It is up to you which method you choose. At first it might be best to try both methods and see which one you like best. Some holy tides have additional things you can do such as Maypole dancing. These will be mentioned here.

Yule

Yule is the highest holy tide of the Anglo-Saxon pagan calendar. It is called Géol in Old English. According to the Christian monk Bede it was when the ancient Anglo-Saxon pagan calendar began:

> The winter festival which Bede called Mothers' Night marked the pagan New Year and was held on 25 December. It is likely that this Yule festival (the pagan name for December and January, we may remember, was giuli) involved the bringing in of evergreens, the burning of a Yule log and a feast centered round a boar's head. Since these non-Christian features became associated with the Christmas festival celebrated at that time. (Owen, *The Rites and Religions of the Anglo-Saxons* p. 48)

Most of what we now associate with Christmas probably stemmed from the ancient Yule celebrations. Yule wreathes, gift giving, and wassailing probably all come from pagan roots. Módraniht or "the night of Mothers" was the first night of the Anglo-Saxon pagan year.

Módraniht

Módraniht takes place the night before the winter solstice. Evidence of Módraniht or Mothers' Night remains illusive. Bede is the only one to mention it. No other Anglo-Saxon source mentions it. Yet we are fortunate that we have a similar set of rites mentioned in other Germanic sources. In the Icelandic Sagas there is frequently mentioned the Dísablót. Most sources have Dísablót as taking place at Winter Nights, the last two days of Fall and first day of Winter in the Icelandic calendar. Winter Nights or *Veturnætur* was the start of the New Year in Iceland, just as Mothers' Night was for the Anglo-Saxons. In some way, the ancient Germanic peoples may have felt that the New Year was somehow sacred to the ancestral mothers. Why? We can only speculate. It may be that they saw it as the birth of the New Year, or that the ancestral women were seen as guarding the home, and therefore called on during the harsh winter months. This link between goddesses and the New Year is apparently not limited to the Anglo-Saxons and Norse. A perusal of Grimm's "Teutonic Mythology" shows that the Yule tide was sacred in someway to several Goddesses. Among them were Peratha:

> It still remains for us to explain her precise connection with a particular day of the year. It is either on Dec. 25 (dies natalis), or twelve days after Christmas, on Jan. 6, when the star appeared to the Three Kings (magi), that the Christian church celebrates the feast of the

manifestation of Christ under the name of epiphania (v. Ducange, sub v.), bethphania or theophania (O. Fr. tiephaine, tiphagne). In an OHG. gloss (Emm. 394), theophania is rendered giperahta naht, the bright night of the heavenly vision that appeared to the shepherds in the field. Documents of the Mid. Ages give dates in the dative case: 'perchtentag, perhtennaht' (for OHG. zi demo perahtin taga, zi deru Perahtûn naht); again, 'an der berechtnaht,' M. Beham (Mone, anz. 4, 451); 'ze perhnahten,' MB. 8, 540 (an. 1302); 'unze an den ahtodin tac nâh der Perhtage,' till the eighth day after the Perht's (fem.) day, Fundgr. 110, 22; 'von dem nehsten Berhtag,' MB. 9, 138 (an. 1317); 'an dem Prehentag,' MB. 7, 256 (an. 1349);—these and other contracted forms are cited with references in Scheffer's Haltaus p. 75, and Schm. 1, 194. Now from this there might very easily grow up a personification, Perchtentac, Perchtennaht, the bright day becoming Bright's, i.e., dame Bright's, day. (Conrad of Dankrotsheim, p. 123, puts his milde Behte down a week earlier, on Dec. 30.) (Stallybrass (tr.) . Grimm, Teutonic Mythology, Chapter 13)

It is easy to note here that the days given, as being in connection with her are Dec. 25, the old date under the Julian calendar for Mothers' Night, or Twelfth Night, on or around New Year's Day under the Gregorian calendar. Both could point to the goddess being linked to the start of the New Year. Yule is also sacred to Holda:

> Her annual progress, which like those of

> Herke and Berhta, is made to fall between Christmas and Twelfth-day, when the supernatural has sway, and wild beasts like the wolf are not mentioned by their names, brings fertility to the land. Not otherwise does 'Derk with the boar,' that Freyr of the Netherlands (p. 214), appear to go his rounds and look after the ploughs. At the same time Holda, like Wuotan, can also ride on the winds, clothed in terror, and she, like the god, belongs to the 'wutende heer.' From this arose the fancy, that witches ride in Holla's company (ch. XXXIV, snowwives); it was already known to Burchard, and now in Upper Hesse and the Westerwald, Holle-riding, to ride with Holle, is equivalent to a witches' ride. (Stallybrass (tr.), Grimm, Teutonic Mythology, Chapter 13, page 5)

Other goddesses such as Beratha and Herke are also seen as holding Yule as a sacred season:

> In the Mark she is called frau Harke, and is said to fly through the country between Christmas and Twelfth-day, dispensing earthly goods in abundance; by Epiphany the maids have to finish spinning their flax, else frau Harke gives them a good scratching or soils their distaff. (Stallybrass (tr.), Grimm, Teutonic Mythology, Chapter 13, page 1)

> With Berahta we have also to consider Holda, Diana and Herodias. Berahta and Holda shew themselves, like frau Gaude (p. 925), in the 'twelves' about New-year's day.(Stallybrass (tr.), Grimm,

Teutonic Mythology, Chapter 31, page 4)

There is, therefore, circumstantial evidence for some sort of rite linked to the goddesses at the start of the New Year amongst the Germanic peoples in what is now Germany. For there not to be some form of rite linked to the above named goddesses in connection with Yule would seem highly unusual.

The Rites

Unfortunately, we have little to no evidence of what rites were performed. We can surmise from the German folk tales that all work was put away during the Twelve Nights. Again and again in folk tales about Holda and Peratha we here that women are not to spin during Yule, that farm implements must be put away, in essence all work for the year must be done. Beyond that, we must go farther abroad for information. Along Hadrian's Wall, in Germany, northern Italy, and modern France there are found altars that were part of the Matron Cult, or Cult of Mothers. Many of these bear Germanic names, although some names are in Latin, and others Gaulish.

More than simple votive stones have been found, however: in some areas there were large cult centers, temples and monuments, especially along the Rhine. Some of the largest were in Pesch, Nettersheim, and Bonn. The temples, monuments and votive stones show that the following were important to the worship of the mothers: -burning bowls of incense -sacrifices of fruit, fish, and pigs, -imagery of fruit baskets, plants, trees, babies, children, cloths for wrapping babies, and snakes. Images of the mothers generally show them in a group of three, though occasionally two or one are found; usually at least one of them holds a basket of fruit, and often a baby is held. Often all of them have clothing and hairstyles or head dressing indicating their matron status, though sometimes the middle figure is shown dressed as a maiden, with her hair loose. (Winifred Hodge, Matrons and Disisr: The Heathen Tribal Mothers retrieved from *http://www.friggasweb.org/matrons.html* on Dec. 4 2006 CE).

These goddesses are given names that relate to "giving" such as Gabiae, Friagabiae, and Alagabiae. From this we can surmise that perhaps the rites consisted of asking the goddesses for prosperity, gifts for the coming new year. The gifts given the goddesses would have consisted of bowls of incense, gifts of fruit, grain, and perhaps even the sacrifice of swine. The Icelandic sagas give us a little more information. In "Egil's Saga," we are told a great feast was held followed by the drinking of many horns of ale (in essence, a symbol). Many became drunk to the point of being sick, and the night ended in the death of Bard at Egil's hands. We are told not much more than that. "Viga-Glums Saga" presents a similar picture. In "Hervarar Saga," the rites were done outdoors at night, and Alfhild, the king's daughter, reddened the altar with blood. Unfortunately, again we are not told much more than that. We can however, figure out from this that both offering and symbol were held, and from the evidence of the cult of Matrons what forms the gifts may have taken.

Conclusion

Using the above information, Mothers' Night can be filled out to include the activities of offering and symbol. We know from the evidence provided by the Matron Cult of the late Roman Empire that incense was burned, and from Norse accounts that some form of animal sacrifice may have taken place. There was more than likely following the offering, a feast, followed by symbel. And all this took place at night with worship taking place outside, but with symbel and feast inside. Bede implies that the rites may have taken the whole of the night, as do the Norse sources. This would have opened the 12 Nights of Yule, but the goddesses were not forgotten after that night. For the rest of the 12 nights certain restrictions applied such as the putting away of work tools and not laboring. If these restrictions were not obeyed, the wrath of the goddesses could be expected.

How you conduct your Mothers' Night celebrations is largely up to you. I usually do an offering to Fríge and the Idesa. The rites I use are similar to the one below. For this rite, you will need your blot bowl, your horn or goblet, a candle, hlót-tán, incense (optional), incense burner (optional), and some mead or wine:

1) The Creation of Sacred Space: Circle the area you will be performing the rite in with a candle and as you are doing it say:

>Fire I bear around the frithyard
>
>And bid all men make peace
>
>Flame I bear to encircle this space
>
>And ask ill wights to fare away
>
>Þunor make sacred, Þunor make sacred
>
>Þunor make sacred this holy site.

2) Hallowing: Pour the mead or wine or other liquid into the horn and blot bowl. You then hallow the food and/or drink by passing them over the flame of the candle or torch. As you are doing this say, "Þunor make sacred this food and drink." If you are using incense, this is a good time to light it. As to what kind of incense you use, that is your choice. Use what

smells good to you. I tend to use raw herbs and usually use a blend of mugwort and white sage.

3) Blessing: You then perform the blessing sprinkling the wine or mead or other drink on yourself and any others present with the hlót-tan.

4) The Prayers: Here you will want to say a prayer to Frige. Below is one I frequently use:

Hail Frige mother, Wóden's mirth,
Dear to the folk, you are light hearted,
Hold secrets and generous are,
Greatness you attain, and for Man counsel know,
Frige all-knowing, cunning goddess,
Ósgeard's queen, pleasing lady.
You guard births, ward the young.
Please protect our families and our children.

5) The Myne or Toasts to the Ancestors: Say the following prayer to the Idesa (the ancestral mothers):

Wassail Idesa, wassail tribal mothers,
Advice you give us, runes and hope,
Forefathers' brides, ring givers' guardians,
Full of life care, dear to families,
Watch over us, and our well-being,
Reward good deeds, and punish wrong ones,
Right's token, steer us true,
Tribal foremothers, teach us thews,
Good harvest and frith, I ask of you.

6) The Housel: At this point you consume part of the food or drink. When you are through drinking from the horn, pour the remaining liquid into the blot bowl.

7) The Yielding: Then if doing the rite indoors take the blot bowl and any other items you are giving outside, and pour it out under a tree with the words, "I give this to Frige and the

Idesa." If you are doing the rite outside, you may pour the drink under a tree, or if using a hearg (stone altar), pour it on it.

Twelve Days of Yule

Some Anglo-Saxon pagans celebrate twelve days of Yule; during this time they do rites to Wóden and Ing, the gods to whom Yuletide is sacred in addition to the tribal mothers. The Twelve Nights of Yule was actually a Christian innovation. We do not know how may days the ancient Anglo-Saxons celebrated Yule. It may have been the entire Anglo-Saxon month of Géol, or only for a few days. We are told in the Norse "Hakon the Good's Saga" in the "Heimskringla" that Yule was celebrated for three days. Twelfth Night or Twelve Nights of Yule are mentioned throughout the "Heimskringla," but always in a Christian context. Twelfth Night is also mentioned in the "Anglo-Saxon Chronicle" for the year 878, but again, this is in a Christian context. Despite this, many, if not most Heathens celebrate twelve nights of Yule. Some folks do something for each of the twelve days. Regardless, most Anglo-Saxon pagans make an offering of Twelfth Night which most years falls on New Year's Eve. The rites vary greatly. Some folks stay up all night while others just stay up until Midnight. To whom the offerings are done vary too. Many Anglo-Saxon pagans make offerings to the gods in general, while other make offerings to Ing or Wóden. I usually do mine to Ing. What follows is a sample rite to Ing for Twelfth Night. The items you will need are a candle, your blot bowl, a hlót-tán, some mead or wine, and your horn or goblet. Feel free to use it.

1) The Creation of Sacred Space: Circle the area you will be performing the rite in with a candle and as you are doing it say:

>Fire I bear around the frithyard
>And bid all men make peace

Flame I bear to encircle this space
And ask ill wights to fare away
Þunor make sacred, Þunor make sacred
Þunor make sacred this holy site.

2) Hallowing: Pour the mead or wine or other liquid into the horn and blot bowl. You then hallow the food and/or drink by passing them over the flame of the candle or torch. As you are doing this say, "Þunor make sacred this food and drink." If you are using incense, this is a good time to light it. As to what kind of incense you use, that is your choice. Use what smells good to you. I tend to use raw herbs and usually use a blend of mugwort and white sage.

3) Blessing: You then perform the blessing sprinkling the wine or mead or other drink on yourself and any others present with the hlót-tan.

4) The Prayers: Here you will want to say a prayer to Ing. Below is one I frequently use:

Wassail Ing, wassail the god of kings,
You were first among the East Danes,
Seen amongst reeds, but you since went eft,
Over the wet way, your wain ran after;
Thus the Heardings named you.
Son of Neord, fresh from the sea,
Tribe's father, warrior's friend,
Wain god, Angles' glory,
Grant us good harvest, grant us good reaping,
Shape into us good men, tribe's god.

5) The Myne or Toasts to the Ancestors: Make a toast to your ancestors.

6) The Housel: At this point you consume part of the food or

drink. When you are through drinking from the horn, pour the remaining liquid into the blot bowl.

7) The Yielding: Then if doing the rite indoors take the blot bowl and any other items you are giving outside, and pour it out under a tree with the words, "I give this to Ing." If you are doing the rite outside, you may pour the drink under a tree, or if using a hearg (stone altar), pour it on it.

Other Yule Traditions

Hoodening

Hoodening is a tradition that was commonly performed in Kent and the Isle of Thanet on Christmas Eve throughout the Middle Ages up to modern times. It is not known if it is pagan in origin, but there are reasons to believe it is. Its details varied some from area to area, but the basic idea is the same. Hoodening consists of carrying either a horse's skull or a wooden representation of one on a pole around house to house. The jaws are rigged so that they can be snapped with the pull of a string. Those accompanying the horse's head dress in skins and carry hand bells or other noise makers. In return for visiting the house they are given gifts. Unless one is a member of a large group hoodening may be impractical.

Morris Dancing

Morris dancing is a type of English dance that consists of rhythmic stepping and choreographed movements. The dancers carry sticks, swords, or even handkerchiefs or bells. Morris dancing is widespread throughout England, and there are Morris teams in the United States as well. Some scholars believe that the dances descend from ancient pagan sword dances that are depicted on some early pagan jewelry. Like hoodening, Morris dancing is impractical for the lone Anglo-Saxon pagan.

Mumming

Mummer plays take place in many parts of England. Unlike hoodening and Morris dancing it is thought that mummer's plays are a late development, and not pagan in origin. Never the less, they are something Heathen groups can do. The plays follow a basic plot that consists of: 1) A hero returns from a distant land. 2) The hero is challenged and killed. 3) A doctor is called and revives the hero. 4) All hostilities are ceased.

Wassailing

Wassailing is the toasting of cherry and apple trees usually on Twelfth Night. It is thought pagan in origin, but has developed over the centuries. Every area of England have their own songs that are sung to the trees, and often guns are shot off. The idea of wassailing is to ensure a good harvest of fruit.

Yule Log

In some areas, a log was brought in, and burned for all twelve nights. Traditions differed from area to area. Generally, the log was started from a coal from the previous year's log. Sometimes the log was garlanded.

Solmónaþ

Solmonaþ takes place in February. Solmonaþ is mentioned in Bede's description of the Anglo-Saxon pagan calendar. According to him, the ancient Anglo-Saxon pagans would bury cakes to the gods in the ground. Many modern Anglo-Saxon pagans celebrate what is called the Blessing of the Plow at this time. Usually, this took place in January in England. Plows would be brought into the churches and blessed. This seems to be a survival of a pagan practice, as the Æcer-Bót contains a plow blessing. However, in most areas in the United States it does not begin to warm up until

February. I usually make my offerings to Eorðe (the earth goddess) at this time. A sample rite for Solmonaþ is below. The items you will need are a small cake, a hoe, a candle, your blot bowl, a hlót-tán, some mead or wine, and your horn or goblet. This rite is meant to be performed outside. Feel free to use it.

1) Preparation: Dig a hole in your yard or garden.

2) Creation of sacred space: Circle the area you will be performing the rite in with a candle and as you are doing it say:

> Fire I bear around the frithyard
>
> And bid all men make peace
>
> Flame I bear to encircle this space
>
> And ask ill wights to fare away
>
> Þunor make sacred, Þunor make sacred
>
> Þunor make sacred this holy site.

3) Blessing of gifts to be given: Pour the mead or wine into your blot bowl. Pass it over the candle with the words, "Þunor please hallow this drink." Then sprinkle the hoe and the cake with the hlót-tán.

4) The First Bede or Prayer: Say the following prayer (it is adapted from the Æcer-bót:

> Eastwards, I stand, for mercies I pray,
>
> I pray the great dryhten, I pray the powerful lord,
> I pray the holy guardian of heaven-kingdom,
> earth I pray and sky
> and heaven's might and high hall,
> that I may this bede by the gift of Woden

open with my teeth through firm thought,
to call forth these plants for our worldly use,
to fill this land with firm belief.

Erce, Erce, Erce, earth's mother,
May the all-father grant you, the eternal lord,
fields growing and flourishing,
propagating and strengthening,
tall shafts, bright crops,
and broad barley crops,
and white wheat crops,
and all earth's crops.
May the eternal Frea grant him,
and his holy ones, who are in heaven,
that his produce be guarded against any enemies whatsoever,
and that it be safe against any harm at all,
from poisons sown around the land.
Now I bid Woden, who shaped this world,
that there be no speaking-woman nor crafty man
that can overturn these words thus spoken.

6) Ritual Actions: Dig a hole in the earth with the hoe big enough to hold the cake. Place the cake in the hole.

7) The Second Bede or Prayer: Say the following prayer:

Wassail earth, mother of men!
May you be growing in Woden's embrace,

with food filled for the needs of men.

Field full of food for mankind,
bright-blooming, you are blessed
in the holy name of the one who shaped heaven
and the earth on which we live.

8) Yielding: You pour the mead into the hole and then cover it with the following words, "Eorðe, I give this to you."

Hredmónaþ

Hredmónaþ is sacred to the goddess Hreda about whom not much is known. Still, modern Anglo-Saxon pagans do rites to her at this time. I take the viewpoint that she is a victory goddess, and thus honor her as such. Below is a sample rite. For it you will need a candle, your blot bowl, a hlót-tán, some mead or wine, and your horn. Most do their rites to Hreda on either the New Moon or Full Moon of March.

1) The Creation of Sacred Space: Circle the area you will be performing the rite in with a candle and as you are doing it say:

> Fire I bear around the frithyard
>
> And bid all men make peace
>
> Flame I bear to encircle this space
>
> And ask ill wights to fare away
>
> Þunor make sacred, Þunor make sacred
>
> Þunor make sacred this holy site.

2) Hallowing: Pour the mead or wine or other liquid into the horn and blot bowl. You then hallow the food and/or drink by passing them over the flame of the candle or torch. As you

are doing this say, "Þunor make sacred this food and drink." If you are using incense, this is a good time to light it. As to what kind of incense you use, that is your choice. Use what smells good to you. I tend to use raw herbs and usually use a blend of mugwort and white sage.

3) Blessing: You then perform the blessing sprinkling the wine or mead or other drink on yourself and any others present with the hlót-tan.

4) The Prayers: Here you will want to say a prayer to Hreda. Below is one I frequently use:

Wassail Hreda, wassail victory goddess,
Beautiful lady with shining hair,
Fair to look upon you are ruler of winter's chill,
Moving into summer, you give warm winds,
Goddess of transitions smile upon us,
Grant us victory in all we do.

5) The Myne or Toasts to the Ancestors: Make a toast to your ancestors.

6) The Housel: At this point you consume part of the food or drink. When you are through drinking from the horn, pour the remaining liquid into the blot bowl.

7) The Yielding: Then if doing the rite indoors take the blot bowl and any other items you are giving outside, and pour it out under a tree with the words, "I give this to Hreda." If you are doing the rite outside, you may pour the drink under a tree, or if using a hearg (stone altar), pour it on it.

Éosturmónaþ

Éosturmónaþ is sacred to the goddess Éostre and perhaps one of the most popular holy tides in modern Anglo-Saxon paganism. There are many traditions surrounding her holy tide, some of them perhaps dating back to pagan times.

Water drawn from brooks and springs was thought particularly holy if drawn on her day (the Full Moon of the month of April). During the Middle Ages it was said that maidens in white were seen frolicking in the fields on Christian Easter. Eggs and hares are holy to Éostre, and they play a role in the activities of the month. Éosturmónaþ is a time of new beginnings, the first signs of spring. Trees leaf out and the first flowers bloom. Many animals begin to have young at this time. Some of the customs associated with Éosturmónaþ are below:

Bonfires

Many places burned bonfires on Easter. These bonfires had many activities associated with them, among them fire leaping (a practice I advise against due to the obvious dangers). Modern Anglo-Saxons can of course incorporate these into their rites.

Decorations

At Easter in many parts of England up until recently many decorations were put out. Trees, wells, houses, and other things were garlanded. Eggs were often blown out and hung on trees. In the United States this tradition is coming back.

Easter Bunny

The Easter Bunny or Hare is a German tradition that caught on in England and the United States. Hares and rabbits are seen as symbols of fertility and begin having young in the spring. They are very good mothers being very attentive to their young. In parts of England, hare hunts were held at this time.

Easter Eggs

There are many customs associated with Easter eggs and modern Anglo-Saxon pagans have adopted these. If you are with a group, coloring eggs can become a group project. The night before your celebration and offering you can color eggs for the games the next day. Besides Easter egg hunts, egg tossing was also done. If you caught the egg unbroken it was thought a sign of good luck. In the group I worship with we have the opposite tradition. If the egg breaks on you it is though the next year will be a fertile one for you (eggs that break on the ground do not count). Egg rolling is a custom that is observed in parts of England. Eggs are taken to the top of a hill and rolled down. This could be incorporated into a race if you want.

Winter Effigy

Many groups make an effigy of winter at this time and beat it and burn it. In this way, they seek to drive out winter and bring in the spring. This makes a great activity for children.

Below is a sample rite for use with your Easter rites. You will need colored eggs, your blot bowl, a hlót-tán, a bottle of mead or wine, and your horn or goblet. This rite should be performed on the Full Moon of April.

1) The Creation of Sacred Space: Circle the area you will be performing the rite in with a candle and as you are doing it say:

> Fire I bear around the frithyard
>
> And bid all men make peace
>
> Flame I bear to encircle this space
>
> And ask ill wights to fare away
>
> Þunor make sacred, Þunor make sacred

Þunor make sacred this holy site.

2) Hallowing: Pour the mead or wine or other liquid into the horn and blot bowl. Then place the eggs in the blot bowl with the liquid. You then hallow the food and/or drink by passing them over the flame of the candle or torch. As you are doing this say, "Þunor make sacred this food and drink." If you are using incense, this is a good time to light it. As to what kind of incense you use, that is your choice. Use what smells good to you. I tend to use raw herbs and usually use a blend of mugwort and white sage.

3) Blessing: You then perform the blessing sprinkling the wine or mead or other drink on yourself and any others present with the hlót-tán.

4) The Prayers: Here you will want to say a prayer to Ēostre. Below is one I frequently use:

Wassail Ēostre, go well Ēostre,
Goddess of the dawn, bringer of day,
Lady in whitebringing water from the wells,
Beautiful goddess, all pure and good,
Bringing waves of grass after winter's chill.
Goddess of the spring, goddess of dawn,
All clad in white full of right good will,
We beseech you now, with this bede,
Give us wonderful days with your winsome smile.
We ask you now and call on your name,
Give us fertile fields and lives full of love.

5) The Myne or Toasts to the Ancestors: Make a toast to your ancestors.

6) The Housel: At this point you consume part of the food or drink. When you are through drinking from the horn, pour the remaining liquid into the blot bowl.

7) The Yielding: Then if doing the rite indoors take the blot bowl and any other items you are giving outside, and pour it out under a tree with the words, "I give this to Ēostre." If you are doing the rite outside, you may pour the drink under a tree, or if using a hearg (stone altar), pour it on it.

Sumerdæg

Sumerdæg or Walpurgis (*Wælburges in Old English) takes place on the first of May. It was believed that witches rode on the eve of this day in medieval times, and prayers were said for cattle, sheep, and goats. In many areas bonfires were lit. Exactly why it is called Walpurgis is not known. It is believed to have been named for a Christian nun, Saint Walburga, although this is not certain. It could be that the saint was named for a goddess and that is where the name truly derives from. If this is so, Walburga may be a hight name for Fréo.

Love and courting are linked to this holy tide. Many customs relate to courtship rituals, the gift of flowers from suitors to young ladies, the Maypole dance, and different types of love divination being done. This was perhaps the reason for June weddings. A long courtship may have accumulated into final courtship in May followed by a wedding in June. There are several traditions associated with this holiday.

Hobby Horse

The hobby horse is very similar to hoodening described in the entry for Yule. A horse's head (either a skull or wooden representation) is taken around the neighborhood.

May Carols

At one time there were songs pertaining to Mayday. Like Yule, Walpurgis seems to be a time for song.

Maypole

When folks think of Mayday or Walpurgis most think of Maypoles. The earliest accounts of Maypoles show they did not use ribbons. Ribbons tied to the pole were a later development. Some villages in England, and elsewhere have a permanent Maypole erected.

Morris Dancing

Many Morris dances take place in England at this time.

I usually do an offering to Fréo at this time. And what follows is a sample rite to her. Feel free to use or adapt it to your needs. Items needed are your blot bowl, a hlót-tán, your horn or goblet, and a candle or torch.

1) The Creation of Sacred Space: Circle the area you will be performing the rite in with a candle and as you are doing it say:

> Fire I bear around the frithyard
>
> And bid all men make peace
>
> Flame I bear to encircle this space
>
> And ask ill wights to fare away
>
> Þunor make sacred, Þunor make sacred
>
> Þunor make sacred this holy site.

2) Hallowing: Pour the mead or wine or other liquid into the horn and blot bowl. You then hallow the food and/or drink by passing them over the flame of the candle or torch. As you are doing this say, "Þunor make sacred this food and drink." If you are using incense, this is a good time to light it. As to what kind of incense you use, that is your choice. Use what smells good to you. I tend to use raw herbs and usually use a blend of mugwort and white sage.

3) Blessing: You then perform the blessing sprinkling the wine or mead or other drink on yourself and any others present with the hlót-tán.

4) The Prayers: Here you will want to say a prayer to Fréo. Below is one I frequently use:

Wassail Fréo, Noble lady of the Wen,
Holiest queen of witchcraft, victory-charm singer,
With wælcyrigen to war you ride,
From Folkwang you take half the battle slain.
Desirable severe one, our fair lady,
Comliest goddess, cat-like of grace,
Come to us, and kiss us with your main,
Give us love and pleasure,
Grant us health and winsomeness.

5) The Myne or Toasts to the Ancestors: Make a toast to your ancestors.

6) The Housel: At this point you consume part of the food or drink. When you are through drinking from the horn, pour the remaining liquid into the blot bowl.

7) The Yielding: Then if doing the rite indoors take the blot bowl and any other items you are giving outside, and pour it out under a tree with the words, "I give this to Fréo." If you are doing the rite outside, you may pour the drink under a tree, or if using a hearg (stone altar), pour it on it.

Liða

Liða or Midsummer takes place at the summer solstice. It was referred to as Midsummer because the ancient Germanic peoples had only two seasons, winter and summer. Winter began with the fall equinox while summer began with the spring equinox. The main showcase of Liða is the bonfires. Fires are built at this time to celebrate the longest day of the year. Folks stay up all night enjoying the fires.

On Midsummer's Eve folks gather flowers for use in the garlands the next day. Many medicinal herbs are gathered as well as they are thought to be more potent at this time. St. John's Wort, Vervain, Mugwort, Feverfew, and Ruc are all gathered at this time. Yarrow hung at Midsummer is thought to keep one healthy all year.

On Midsummer Day wells, houses, and were decorated in the Middle Ages using the flowers gathered the night before.

Bonfires

Bonfires were probably started by friction using a fire bow or fire drill during the Middle Ages. These tools are used to start what is known as need fire, a fire whose properties are thought to keep away disease. Once the fire is started folks dance around the fire. Leaping through the fire is not unheard of, but unadvisable for obvious reasons.

Burning Wheels

In some parts of England and in Germany during the Middle Ages, wooden wheels would be set on fire and rolled down hills.

I usually perform a rite to Sunne, goddess of the Sun at this time. For the following rite you will need your blot bowl, a hlót-tán, your horn or goblet, and a candle or torch.

1) The Creation of Sacred Space: Circle the area you will be performing the rite in with a candle and as you are doing it say:

> Fire I bear around the frithyard

And bid all men make peace
Flame I bear to encircle this space
And ask ill wights to fare away
Þunor make sacred, Þunor make sacred
Þunor make sacred this holy site.

2) Hallowing: Pour the mead or wine or other liquid into the horn and blot bowl. You then hallow the food and/or drink by passing them over the flame of the candle or torch. As you are doing this say, "Þunor make sacred this food and drink." If you are using incense, this is a good time to light it. As to what kind of incense you use, that is your choice. Use what smells good to you. I tend to use raw herbs and usually use a blend of mugwort and white sage.

3) Blessing: You then perform the blessing sprinkling the wine or mead or other drink on yourself and any others present with the hlót-tán.

4) The Prayers: Here you will want to say a prayer to Sunne. Below is one I frequently use:

Wassail Sunne, wassail Sigel,
All shining day star,
Lovely wheel, fair wheel,
Moon's sister, heaven shine,
Set high in the sky, shining bright,
Lighting the earth, shining down,
Evershine, elfdisk,
Grant us fair skies, give us good harvest,
Grant us shining skies, give us fair seas.

5) The Myne or Toasts to the Ancestors: Make a toast to your ancestors.

6) The Housel: At this point you consume part of the food or

drink. When you are through drinking from the horn, pour the remaining liquid into the blot bowl.

7) The Yielding: Then if doing the rite indoors take the blot bowl and any other items you are giving outside, and pour it out under a tree with the words, "I give this to Sunne." If you are doing the rite outside, you may pour the drink under a tree, or if using a hearg (stone altar), pour it on it.

Hláfmæst

Hláfmæst is a term that Garman Lord came up with for the medieval festival of Lamass. It means "loaf feast" In medieval times Lamass was a celebration of the wheat harvest coming in, as well as the first apples being gathered. While there is no evidence it dates back to a time before the conversion to Christianity, many modern Anglo-Saxon pagans celebrate it.

Lamass was a big deal in medieval England. It was the first harvest of the year. The harvest would be brought in, and harvest dolls made from the stalks of wheat. Apples would be harvested and cider made. This is also the time when the common lands of the villages would be open for grazing cattle, sheep, and goats. Today we celebrate it as a reward for hard work done, for projects finished.

I generally make an offering to Þunor and his wife Sibbe at this time. What follows is typical of the rite I do. For it you will need your blot bowl, a hlót-tán, your horn or goblet, and a candle or torch.

1) The Creation of Sacred Space: Circle the area you will be performing the rite in with a candle and as you are doing it say:

> Fire I bear around the frithyard
> And bid all men make peace

Flame I bear to encircle this space
And ask ill wights to fare away
Þunor make sacred, Þunor make sacred
Þunor make sacred this holy site.

2) Hallowing: Pour the mead or wine or other liquid into the horn and blot bowl. You then hallow the food and/or drink by passing them over the flame of the candle or torch. As you are doing this say, "Þunor make sacred this food and drink." If you are using incense, this is a good time to light it. As to what kind of incense you use, that is your choice. Use what smells good to you. I tend to use raw herbs and usually use a blend of mugwort and white sage.

3) Blessing: You then perform the blessing sprinkling the wine or mead or other drink on yourself and any others present with the hlót-tán.

4) The Prayers: Here you will want to say a prayer to Þunor. Below is one I frequently use:

Wassail Þunor, Wassail Earth' son,
You went fishing for Middeneard's wyrm,
It reared its head and hammer smashed down,
You slew "Great-wand," great warder of Mankind,
With your mighty sledge, you smashed its brains.
You smashed the limbs of Leiken, you smashed Trivaldi,
You knocked down Starkad, and tread Gjalp under foot.
Holy Hallower, High in Heaven,
Ward us with your might, ward us with your main.

5) The Myne or Toasts to the Ancestors: Make a toast to your ancestors.

6) The Housel: At this point you consume part of the food or drink. When you are through drinking from the horn, pour the remaining liquid into the blot bowl.

7) The Yielding: Then if doing the rite indoors take the blot bowl and any other items you are giving outside, and pour it out under a tree with the words, "I give this to Þunor." If you are doing the rite outside, you may pour the drink under a tree, or if using a hearg (stone altar), pour it on it.

Háligmónaþ

Háligmónaþ is in September, and mentioned by the Christian monk Bede. Other than that we do not know why the month was holy. It is the time when many modern Anglo-Saxon pagans celebrate Harvest Home. Harvest falls in the middle of the harvests for many areas, at the end for others. Like Lamass, it had many activities associated with it in medieval England. Harvest dolls were made, and there were even harvest songs like the well-known song "John Barleycorn." I usually honor Ing at this time. And the following sample rite is typical of what I do. For it you will need your blot bowl, a hlót-tán, your horn or goblet, and candle or torch.

1) The Creation of Sacred Space: Circle the area you will be performing the rite in with a candle and as you are doing it say:

>Fire I bear around the frithyard
>
>And bid all men make peace
>
>Flame I bear to encircle this space
>
>And ask ill wights to fare away
>
>Þunor make sacred, Þunor make sacred
>
>Þunor make sacred this holy site.

2) Hallowing: Pour the mead or wine or other liquid into the horn and blot bowl. You then hallow the food and/or drink

by passing them over the flame of the candle or torch. As you are doing this say, "Þunor make sacred this food and drink." If you are using incense, this is a good time to light it. As to what kind of incense you use, that is your choice. Use what smells good to you. I tend to use raw herbs and usually use a blend of mugwort and white sage.

3) Blessing: You then perform the blessing sprinkling the wine or mead or other drink on yourself and any others present with the hlót-tán.

4) The Prayers: Here you will want to say a prayer to Ing. Below is one I frequently use:

I bow to you Wen's leader,
Song and boast I sing to you,
Ing Froda; Fréa almighty,
Through fields fared your wain,
In olden days frith fullfilled,
Children leaped through flowers,
And lovers laid in meadows,
As earls sang seated at symble,
Queens spoke pleasing words.
Summer draws on plows in the field,
Just as the ancestors in days of old,
Today we place faith in you,
Worship you Wen king,
The Ésa protector almighty Ing.
Wassail world's god,
Wassail Ing In your embrace Gerd grows,
Bright blooming With child,
Vanir child, the world's blooming.
Bless Us; eternal Ing!

5) The Myne or Toasts to the Ancestors: Make a toast to your ancestors.

6) The Housel: At this point you consume part of the food or drink. When you are through drinking from the horn, pour

the remaining liquid into the blot bowl.

7) The Yielding: Then if doing the rite indoors take the blot bowl and any other items you are giving outside, and pour it out under a tree with the words, "I give this to Ing." If you are doing the rite outside, you may pour the drink under a tree, or if using a hearg (stone altar), pour it on it.

Winterfylleþ

Winterfylleþ falls in October. There is no indication that an Anglo-Saxon festival fell at this time. For the Norse there was Winter Nights, which was a festival of the ancestors. For that reason many Anglo-Saxon pagans celebrate it. Others wait until November and celebrate Blótmónaþ for which there is evidence of an Anglo-Saxon festival. Many modern Anglo-Saxon pagans combine Winterfylleþ with Halloween celebrations and customs.

I honor the ancestors at this time, and use the following rite to do so. For this you will need your blot bowl, a hlót-tán, your horn or goblet, and a candle or torch.

1) The Creation of Sacred Space: Circle the area you will be performing the rite in with a candle and as you are doing it say:

> Fire I bear around the frithyard
>
> And bid all men make peace
>
> Flame I bear to encircle this space
>
> And ask ill wights to fare away
>
> Þunor make sacred, Þunor make sacred
>
> Þunor make sacred this holy site.

2) Hallowing: Pour the mead or wine or other liquid into the horn and blot bowl. You then hallow the food and/or drink

by passing them over the flame of the candle or torch. As you are doing this say, "Þunor make sacred this food and drink." If you are using incense, this is a good time to light it. As to what kind of incense you use, that is your choice. Use what smells good to you. I tend to use raw herbs and usually use a blend of mugwort and white sage.

3) Blessing: You then perform the blessing sprinkling the wine or mead or other drink on yourself and any others present with the hlót-tán.

4) The Prayers: Here you will want to say a prayer to the ancestors. Below is one I frequently use:

Wassail Idesa, wassail elves,
Godspeed the forebearers, I sing to you!
Dance around the graves and praise Wóden,
Fare through the skies singing death songs,
Sing for the dead and good gifts and glorious words.
Souls of ancient days, the tribe's folkmain,
Ward us spiritually from within your tombs,
Just as the holy ones you are, the heroes you were.
Ancient kin I bid you, enjoy our hospitality,
And bring wit and wisdom, great might and main.

5) The Myne or Toasts to the Ancestors: Make a toast to a specific ancestor or ancestors.

6) The Housel: At this point you consume part of the food or drink. When you are through drinking from the horn, pour the remaining liquid into the blot bowl.

7) The Yielding: Then if doing the rite indoors take the blot bowl and any other items you are giving outside, and pour it out under a tree with the words, "I give this to my ancestors." If you are doing the rite outside, you may pour the drink under a tree, or if using a hearg (stone altar), pour it on it.

Conclusion

One can celebrate many other holy tides as they see fit. There is no reason one cannot make offerings on national holidays or on significant dates. For example, my group does an offering to King Penda on or around November 15th, the anniversary of his death. Too, one can perform many minor rites throughout the year. Offerings to the elves and ancestors can be done at anytime and you may want to do these on a regular schedule, say the first Sunday or every month or other time. One need not celebrate all the holy tides listed here. They are only suggestions of the most common ones among modern Anglo-Saxon pagans. Not all modern Anglo-Saxon pagans celebrate all of them. Others celebrate holy tides not listed here. Finally, feel free to use the rites listed here. Modify them as you see fit, add prayers, rewrite the prayers listed here, do as you want with them.

Endword

Now that you have read this book, it is time to begin your worship of the Anglo-Saxon gods and goddesses (if that was your intent for reading this book) if you have not already. It will be a long path, and you will never stop learning. For some, this book will be enough. For others, this book will merely be a starting point. It is suggested you obtain and read the books in the suggested reading list, and then move onto reading the books in the bibliography if you wish to continue to learn. Even if you decide this book is enough for you to worship the Anglo-Saxon gods, and that you need not do more reading, you will never stop learning. Each time you interact with the gods and goddesses you will learn something. Ours is a living religion with living gods and goddesses. They interact with us, speak to us, and guide us through our daily lives. I think though as you continue to practice Anglo-Saxon paganism you will want to read more. Indeed, even after all these years I am still reading books on Anglo-Saxon paganism. New scholarly books on the Anglo-Saxons come out all the time, and I feel I must stay current.

With luck you will find a group to worship with. If not, then it is perfectly fine to worship by your self. I went many years with only my brother to worship with before finding others. If you are seeking to find others to worship with the Internet is a great place to start. There are Anglo-Saxon groups on most of the social networking sites, not to mention mailing lists, and discussion boards elsewhere. Outside of the Internet you may wish to attend pagan gatherings to seek out other Heathens. Sometimes you may find another Heathen there seeking others as well. Pagan Pride Days and other such events are a perfect place to find other Heathens. You may also want to ask around at pagan bookstores. Often the owners or folks that work there may know of Heathen groups in the area.

Finally, I hope you enjoyed this book, and want to

read more. I cannot stress enough reading the books in the suggested reading list. You will also find many gems in the bibliography. If you have questions you can email me at swain@englatheod.org

Glossary

Ælf: An elf.

Bede: A prayer. Sometimes spelt bedu or gebed.

Blót: The ritual slaughter of an animal to be shared between gods and men. The animal is slain, butchered, and prepared for feast. A portion of the meat is then offered to the gods and goddesses. Sometimes used in Asatru to mean any offering.

Dweorg: A member of a race of beings that live beneath the earth, and are expert smiths

Ésatreow: Faith in the Ése. Sometimes used of Anglo-Saxon paganism.

Ése: A family of gods and goddesses including among them Wóden, Fríge, Tiw, and Þunor

Faining: A day of celebration connected with an offering. Sometimes it is used to mean the offering its self.

Fægning: Old English for faining.

Frith: The peace and security enjoyed within a group.

Frithstead: A holy site used for performing offerings. Sometimes ropes, a fence, or some other means are used to mark off the enclosed area.

Friþgeard: An Old English word meaning the same thing as frithstead.

Frithyard: Same as frithstead.

Galdor: A spoken magical charm or spell.

Gield: Old English noun for an offering or sacrifice. Sometimes spelled gyld or gild.

Gieldan: Old English verb for "to make an offering or sacrifice."

God Post: An idol made from the trunk of a tree and used outside for worship. Sometimes, smaller ones are used indoors.

Grith: Peace between groups.

Hearg: Old English for an outdoor altar made of stone.

Harrow: An outdoor altar made of stone.

Hörg: Old Norse for an outdoor altar of stone.

Housel: A sacred feast, it is also the portion of an offering where mead or other liquid, and/or food are consumed.

Húsel: Old English for a sacred feast, it is also the portion of an offering where mead or other liquid, and/or food are consumed.

Idesa: The ancestral mothers.

Innangarðs: Old Norse for all that is inside an enclosure both literally such as in a frithstead or home and figuratively such as in a tribe.

Inneryard: An enclosure both literally such as in a frithstead, and figuratively such as in a tribe.

Lore: The cumulative knowledge of the gods and goddess, rites, and beliefs of the ancient Heathens as preserved in texts and archaeological finds.

Main: Spiritual might or power, strength.

Minni: Old Norse for the toast made to the ancestors during an offering or symbel.

Mimer's Well: A well belonging to a being known as Mimer to which Wóden sacrificed one of his eyes for wisdom.

Moot: A gathering of Heathens or meeting. It can also refer to a formal assembly.

Myne: Old English for the toast made to the ancestors during an offering or symbel.

Offering: A sacrifice.

Orlæg: One's destiny or fate as laid down by the Wyrdæ and/or the gods and goddesses.

Offerung: Old English for an offering or sacrifice. It is a borrowed word from Latin.

Óðroerir: Old Norse name for the mead of inspiration which was stolen back from the giants by the god Wóden.

Outeryard: All that is outside an enclosure be it literally as in a frithstead or home, or figuratively as in a tribe.

Récels: Raw herbs burned like incense for rites.

Rede: Advice.

Rune: A sacred letter in the ancient Anglo-Saxon alphabet.

Symbel: A rite consisting of ritual toasts to the gods, goddesses, and ancestors as well as boasts and oaths to do great things.

Thew: A virtue or custom.

Úttangarðs: Old Norse for all that is outside an enclosure be it literally as in a frithstead or home, or figuratively as in a tribe.

Wen: A family of gods that includes Ing and his sister Fréo. Wen is a reconstructed word based on the Norse Vanir. It is not attested to in Old English.

Wéofod: An altar.

Wéofodthane or Wéofodþane: An Anglo-Saxon pagan priest.

Wéoh: A statue or carving of a god or goddesses used in rituals and resting upon an altar.

Werman: A human male.

Wight: Any spiritual being, this includes elves, gods, dwarves, giants, and men. Usually though it is used of lesser beings.

Wild Hunt: A spectral hunt consisting of ghosts lead by the god Wóden that gathers lost souls.

Wort: an herb.

Wyrd: One's fate as formed by their actions; the results of actions. It is also the name of the main goddess of fate.

Wyrdæ: The three sisters responsible for determining one's fate or destiny.

Yield: A sacrifice.

Greetings

Wassail: "Be whole, healthy."

Wes hál: Old English for "be whole, healthy"

Welgá: Old English for "Go well."

Suggested Reading List

Scholarly Works

"Culture of the Teutons" by Vilhelm Grönbech, published by Createspace

"Heathen Gods in Old English Literature" by Richard North, published by Cambridge University Press.

"Looking for the Lost Gods of England" by Kathleen Herbert, published by Anglo-Saxon Books

"The Lost Gods of England" by Brian Branston, published by Constable.

"Rites and Religions of the Anglo-Saxons" by Gale Owen, published by Barnes & Noble.

"Teutonic Mythology" volumes 1-4 by Jacob Grimm, James Steven Stallybrass (translator), published by Nabu Press.

"The Elder Gods: The Otherworld of Early England" by Stephen Pollington, published by Anglo-Saxon Books

Heathen Books

"Hammer of the Gods: Anglo-Saxon Paganism in Modern Times" by Swain Wódening, published by Createspace.

"Travels through Middle Earth: the Path of a Saxon Pagan" by Alaric Albertsson, published by Llewellyn Publications.

"We are Our Deeds: the Elder Heathenry, Its Ethic and Thew" by Eric Wódening, published by White Marsh Theod.

"Wyrd Words: A Collection of Essays on Germanic Heathenry" by Swain Wódening, published by Createspace.

Internet Resouces

Wednesbury Shire of White Marsh Theod
http://www.englatheod.org

ASHmail (Anglo-Saxon Heathen Mail): A Yahoo Group for the discussion of Anglo-Saxon Heathenry.
http://groups.yahoo.com/group/ASHMAIL/

Ealdríce Hæðengyld
http://ealdrice.org

Bibliography

Aswynn, Freya. Leaves of Yggdrasil. (St. Paul, MN: Llewellyn)
Bauschatz, Paul. The Well and the Tree (Amherst, MA: University of Massachusetts Press, 1982)
Blain, Jenny Nine Worlds of Seid-Magic: Ecstasy and Neo-Shamanism in North European Paganism, (Routledge, 2001)
Bosworth, Joseph; T.Northcote Toller. An Anglo-Saxon Dictionary and An Anglo-Saxon Dictionary: Supplement. (Oxford, England: Oxford University Press).
Branston, Brian. Gods of the North (London: Thames & Hudson, 1955)
Branston, Brain. Lost Gods of England (London: Thames and Hudson)
Byock, Jesse (tr.). Saga of the Volsungs. (Berkeley, CA : University of California Press)
Cæsar, Julius; S.A. Handford, tr. The Conquest of Gaul (Penguin Books, 1982).
Chisholm, James, Grove and Gallows (Austin TX: Rune-Gild, 1987).
Cleasby, Richard; Gudbrand Vigfusson, An Icelandic-English Dictionary (Oxford, England: Oxford University Press)
Conquergood, Dwight. "Boasting in Anglo-Saxon England, Performance, and the Heroic Ethos". Literature and Performance, vol. I, April 1991, pp. 24-35.
DaSant, George W.(tr.) Njal's Saga ((London, 1861) Elliot, R.W.V. Runes, (Manchester, England: Manchester University Press)
Ellis-Davidson, H.R. Gods and Myths of Northern Europe. (New York, NY: Viking-Penguin)
Ellis-Davidson, H.R. Myths and Symbols in Pagan Europe. (New York: University of Syracuse Press: Syracuse).
Ellis, H.R. The Road to Hel (Cambridge: Cambridge University Press, 1943; rep. Greenwood Press, 1977).
Gloseki, Stephen. Shamanism and Old English Poetry (New York: Garland Publishing, 1989).
Grammaticus, Saxo; Oliver Elton (tr.) The Danish History

(Norroena Society, 1905).
Grattan, John Henry Grafton. and Charles Singer. Anglo-Saxon Magic and Medicine (Norwood, PA: Norwood Editions, 1976).
Griffiths, Bill, Aspects of Anglo-Saxon Magic (Norfolk: Anglo-Saxon Books, 1999)
Grimm, Jacob; James Stallybrass (tr.) Teutonic Mythology (4 vols). (Magnolia, MA: Peter Smith Publishing) Grönbech, Vilhelm. Culture of the Teutons (London: Oxford University Press, 1931).
Gundarsson., Kveldulf Teutonic Religion (St. Paul, MN: Llewellyn,1996)
Hastrup, Kirsten. Culture and History in Mediæval Iceland (Oxford: Clarendon Press, 1985)
Hall, Alaric, Elves in Anglo-Saxon England (Woodbridge, England: Boydell Press, 2009)
Hallakarva , Gunnora "Courtship, Love and Marriage in Viking Scandinavia" (http://viskinganswerlady.org [Electronic version])
Hodge, Winifred, "On the Meaning of Frith" (Lina, Midsummer 1996)
Hollander, Lee. The Poetic Edda. (Austin, TX: University of Texas Press)
Lang, Samuel (tr.) Heimskringla: A History of the Norse Kings (London: Norroena Society, 1907)
Owen, Gale R. Rites and Religions of the Anglo-Saxons (Dorset Press, 1985)
Page, R.I. An Introduction to English Runes, (London: Methuen and Co.)
Paxson, Diana, "The Matronæ" (Sage Woman, Fall, 1999)
Paxson, Diana "The Return of the Völva: Recovering the Practice of Seidh (Mountain Thunder, Summer, 1993)
Polomé, Edgar C. Essays on Germanic Religion (Washington: Institute for the Study of Man, 1989).
Press, Muriel (tr.) Laxdaela Saga (London: The Temple Classics, 1899)
Schwartz, Stephen P. Poetry and Law in Germanic Myth (Berkeley: University of California Press, 1973)
Storms, Anglo-Saxon Magic (The Hague: Martinus Nijhoff,

1948)
Shaw, Philip A. Pagan Goddesses in the Early Germanic World: Eostre, Hreda, and the Cult of Matrons (London: Bristol Classical Press, 2011)
Sturluson, Snorri ; Anthony Faulkes (tr.). Edda. (Rutland VT : Everyman's Press)
Snorri Sturluson; Erling Monsen, A.H. Smith (trs., eds). Heimskringla. (New York, NY: Dover Publications: Inc).
Storms, Dr. G. Anglo-Saxon Magic (The Hague: Martinus Nijhoff, 1948).
Tacitus, Cornelius. Agricola, Germania, Dialogus. Loeb Classics Library ed., (Cambridge, MA: Harvard University Press)
Thorsson, Edred, A Book of Troth (St. Paul, MN: Llewellyn)
Turville-Petre, E.O.G. Myth and Religion of the North. (Westport, CT: Greenwood Publishing Group)
Wilson, David. Anglo-Saxon Paganism (New York, NY: Routledge, 1992)
Wilson, David M. (ed.) The Archaeology of Anglo-Saxon England (Cambridge: University Press, 1981)
Wodening, Eric, "The Meaning of Frith" (Ásatrú Today, December 1994)
Wodening, Eric, We Are Our Deeds: The Elder Heathenry, its Ethic and Thew (Watertown, NY: THEOD, 1998)
Wodening, Swain, Beyond Good and Evil: Germanic Heathen Ethics (Watertown, NY: THEOD, 1994)
Wodening, Swain, Þéodpisc Geléfa" The Belief of the Tribe (Huntsville, MO: Englatheod, 2007)

Printed in Great Britain
by Amazon